MARIA S. ED

LIVING ON
FAITH
Grace &
BONFIRES

a true story...

ISBN:
978-1-68489-894-7 (Paperback)
978-1-68489-883-1 (Ebook)

www.FaithGraceBonfires.com

CONTENTS

Ruth Goff

LIVING ON FAITH, GRACE & BONFIRES

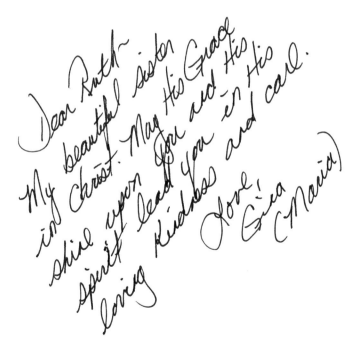

Dear Ruth~
My beautiful sister
in Christ. May His Grace
shine upon you and His
Spirit lead you in His
loving kindness and care.
love!
Erica
(Maria)

To those whom I love
The better part of my story
My heart above all things

To the one who asked
So long ago
To write and spread my wings

To the Green family
Who endured the cost
Leaving a faithful legacy

For Mandy
Miracle child
Strength of the heavenly

To Stephen, who tested these words
With fire and pen
My editor, writing partner and friend

And to the ONE
The True Author
Eternal and unfailing

Who gave me words
A psalm or two
And His spirit of love abiding

in gratitude...
Maria

1

TRIAL BY FAITH

"And there are also many other things that Jesus did, which if they were written one by one, I suppose that even the world itself could not contain the books that would be written. Amen."

— JOHN 21:25 NKJV

What if you and your family were offered a sacred mission? One that would require 4 ½ to 5 years of faithful commitment to it and leave no room for error. Your faith would be put to the test on a daily basis for months, extending into years, with no clear or present end in sight. No guarantee of success would be offered. You would face unanticipated battles daily and your heart would break in places that you never knew existed. Along the journey, you could lose everything you own, yet, you will not walk alone. Would you accept this mission? You may be wondering, "What would I receive if I succeed?" or, "What is at stake?" What if your child's life, or the life of someone you love, depended on your acceptance of the mission?

The extraordinary true story and events of one family's journey are told in this book. Clarence and Beverly Green, along with their children, embarked on a mission to keep their daughter Mandy alive, no matter the cost. They did not ask for this mission. There were no assurances given that their daughter would survive. The only certainty would be the financial challenge of raising their six children, at the end of the mission, while in a state of financial catastrophe.

Who would you turn to for help, guidance and solace?

Who can offer hope when all visible evidence supports the reality of the fears that consume your mind, soul and very spiritual being? What source of comfort will we seek when answers cannot be found in worldly wisdom or in the hands of men?

The eternal 'book', is a word by word account of the history of God and his people. Its pages are threaded together, inextricably bound by the hand of God and impossible to disentangle. It is His truth that sets us free. We ask ourselves, what are the 'many other things' spoken of in this passage? Our lives, woven together, contain the greater story of the many things which Jesus did.Thousands of years after Jesus began his ministry, we see His hand at work in the Green family's story. We are now part of something unexpected. As we follow their story, we experience the emotions of parents and a family whose child was at death's door too many times to count. Perhaps, like Clarence, Mandy's father, you will wonder at times, "Where is God?"

We are offered a lens through which we witness the evidence of God's real and active presence in the lives of His children - and perhaps, we will come to recognize it as our own experience. In this way, the Greens' story speaks to each one of us, connects us to one another, and is a continuing chapter in His eternal, never ending story. We, His children, are the story that is still being written. Each day brings with it the opportunity to witness and testify to the "many other things" that John spoke of. The powerful truth is that we become bound to one another - and we discover that we are far more alike than we are different.

None of us are exempt from the difficulties of life. There will be moments when we will feel as though no one understands. We will feel alone. We won't see a way out. During those times, comfort comes in remembering. Remember that the trail of faith has been blazed by those who have gone before us in battle and trial; and who have won the victory. We are not alone. We are not the first. We won't be the last. We follow in the footsteps of generations of God's children who have endured seemingly impossible challenging moments in their lives. From warriors to poets, and the young and the old. Good people, great people, mighty people, weak people, rich people and poor people have been put to the test. Some had faith that was outspoken and bold, full of zeal. Others had quiet faith that was steadfast and calm; the size of the tiniest mustard seed. But one truth has remained constant through the ages, God's love. His active presence in the lives of His children and His promise of deliverance from these moments cannot be denied.

There are times in our lives when all we can do is cry out and ask, "Why?!" It is not always clear or fully revealed to us, yet God's purpose is certain and we are assured as His children that the end of our story will work together for good. Yet, still, God's goodness is not measured in earthly terms. Clarence and Beverly Green trusted and drew strength from the God they chose to serve and the call they answered in the days of their youth. However, if you were to ask them if it felt good to live under the constant, daily threat of losing their precious child, Mandy, they would say that it was a traumatic, heart wrenching test of their faith.

I would be willing to bet that many of us have experienced the same feelings of fear and doubt as a result of our own trials. Naturally, our first choice would be to "skip through the rough stuff, the tough stuff, or the heartbreaks of life." What we would "prefer" for ourselves on this journey through life often looks very different from where God leads us. It has been my experience that standing in the fires of challenge become moments of choice. Moments when we choose to be in God's will, although we cannot see past our circumstance. When we cannot see the reason for God's action or perceived inaction, when we can't see past a present, uncertain moment in time, we are assured by His word that there is purpose in all these events. His presence remains. The same God who holds the stars, holds us in the palms of His hands. We are treasured and loved by the One who created us in His image. The assurance that God is who He says He is, and the promise that He will do what He has said He will do, is our foundation of faith. Through trials and circumstances, He is present, carrying us beneath the shadow of His wings, offering true refuge from the storms of this life. The Green family survived the unthinkable by remaining faithful to these words, living each day beneath wings of assurance and promise.

2

MOMENT BY MOMENT

"Because thy lovingkindness is better than life, my lips shall praise thee."

— PSALM 63:3 (NKJV)

Our lives are filled with wondrous moments. Moments that take our breath away and moments we hold our breath through. Some moments are designed for a particular purpose - a purpose with far reaching and life changing implications. There will be other moments in our lives when we are invited to stand on holy ground and witness God's hand at work in a wonderful, magnificent way; and we will be called upon to rise up and sing His praises. When the hand of God moves swiftly, these moments are revealed with such piercing clarity, that all who witness them understand - they are standing in His presence.

With this understanding, we acknowledge that we are a witness to something greater than ourselves. We are playing a part in a larger story - beyond what our eyes can see and what our hearts are able to conceive. People and places, coming together, acting in precise harmony to form what some refer to as perfect timing; a divine appointment, and the authorship of these moments is revealed. There are no coincidences. We are able to look back and clearly witness the imprint of God's Hand that moved, designed and set these events into motion. If we willingly seek Him, God is faithful to comfort us in His presence and reveal the moments that He has authored in our lives.

Think about it. What if we approached each day as though it were a heavenly appointment from our Creator? Webster's Revised Unabridged Dictionary defines "appointment" this way, "The act of appointing; designation of a person to hold an office or discharge a trust." In other words, one who is chosen for a purpose ahead of time; designated and entrusted to his or her appointment with confidence. When the One who sets the "appointment" is God, we can view it as a Divine Trust. Consider the idea that each day, our lives have been designated or appointed to fulfill God's Divine Trust. Our lives and the moments that shape them are authored by Him, and are not a coincidence.

There will be happenings and occurrences in our lives that we will naturally want to question. It has been my experience that those events have to do with sorrow, trials, pain, betrayal, tragedy or loss. These are the difficulties that call upon us to weather the storm, not knowing what lies ahead. When there is no hope left and circumstances tear at us from all directions, the comfort of God's Word suddenly becomes alive, active and real in such a tangible way that it becomes our main source of strength, along with a heavenly weapon; prayer. When circumstances are beyond understanding, we can be comforted by *Romans 8:35. "Who shall separate us from the love of Christ? Shall tribulation, or distress, or persecution, or famine, or nakedness, or peril, or sword?"* And God goes on to say in verses *37-39*, *"Yet in all these things we are more than conquerors through Him who loved us. For I am persuaded that neither death nor life, nor angels nor principalities nor powers, nor things present nor things to come, nor height nor depth, nor any other created thing, shall be able to separate us from the love of God which is in Christ Jesus our Lord."* *(KJV)* We are assured through His Word that there is no moment in our life larger or greater than our God, and, most certainly, His grace is sufficient to carry us through any earthly crisis.

NO GUARANTEES

"O Lᴏʀᴅ, how long will you forget me?
Forever?
How long will you look the other way?
How long must I struggle with anguish in my soul,
with sorrow in my heart every day?"

— PSALM 13:1-2 NLT

The rocking chair kept a steady, smooth rhythm. Beverly glanced at the monitors in the dimly lit room. The bleeps and lights indicated that Mandy was stable. She checked her watch again, 7:45am. "Clarence should be getting back soon." She squirmed, adjusting the pillow beneath her neck for the tenth time and attempted to lay the thin blanket evenly across her legs, trying to get comfortable. Once settled, on cue, her rocking resumed. Beverly blinked back the sleep she longed for and shook her head in disbelief. This scene was all too familiar. The cramped room, the sterile feel and stale air, the ugly monitor and lights that could never be dimmed enough to get a good night of sleep, were a constant. Once again, they were praying Mandy back to life. Beverly refused to believe that God saved Mandy, only to take her from them now. "There's just no way," Beverly said, continuing her conversation as she looked at her daughter. The doctors warned, "She's going to be swollen from the process of cleansing her blood throughout the surgery." That was an understatement. Had she not been told it was Mandy, she might not have recognized her daughter. The doctor saw the worry on the faces of her parents. He also was aware of their deep faith in God. "Mandy is a champ," he said. "But she lost about 17 units of blood during surgery which is more than she had in her body. She is having difficulty coming out of the anesthesia." "She was in surgery for double the amount of time anticipated, so this is to be expected." He looked away for a moment, then back to Clarence and Beverly. The loud silence in the room spoke volumes. There was a pause in the Doctor's words. "I'm sorry. Nothing at this point is guaranteed. I suggest you go home, rest and come back in the morning." Clarence looked at Beverly. He knew his wife would not be leaving the hospital. "I'll take the kids home and come back in the morning." There would be no negotiation on that point.

The corridor that led to the ICU was quiet the next morning as Clarence turned the corner. He passed the nurse's station with a quick nod and forced smile as he kept his pace. He stopped short outside Mandy's room, took a deep breath and let it out as he gently pushed open the door. He glanced at his wife, gently rocking, eyes closed; most likely praying, not sleeping. He surveyed the room. A giant stuffed Minnie Mouse, tightly tucked in the corner chair with a hospital blanket, looked like it was settled in for the long haul. He swallowed hard, staring at Mandy. He felt powerless. He placed his hand gently on Beverly's shoulder as she opened her eyes. "Good morning," he managed to choke out as he bent to kiss her forehead. Beverly smiled. "Minnie took your chair." No conversation about Mandy was necessary. They were both well aware of the battle to come.

CODE BLUE

"In heavenly love abiding, no change my heart shall fear;
and safe is such confiding, for nothing changes here:
the storm may roar without me, my heart may low be laid;
but God is round about me, and can I be dismayed?"

— IN HEAVENLY LOVE ABIDING: ANNA LETITIA
WARING - 1850

"Melody Green, please report to the principal's office." The announcement crackled through the outdated speaker on the teacher's desk. Melody kept working as the teacher looked her way. "Melody Green to the principal's office," the voice again beckoned. Melody jumped out of her chair, as her teacher nodded with permission. Quickly grabbing her books and supplies, she turned in her last exam of the year and bolted out the door paying no attention to the stares of her classmates. Her brother Woody was waiting in the principal's office as Melody rushed in, breaking through the administrative silence, dropping her books and papers. "We have to get Molly from school and get to the hospital," Woody said as he hurriedly helped Melody pick up her things. "It's not good. They don't think Mandy is going to make it."

"Hurry up Woody!" Melody cried from the passenger seat of the car, panicking. Woody glanced at Molly in the rearview mirror. "You ok?" Molly nodded from the back seat, wide eyed, fighting back tears. "We'll get there, Melody." Woody said, eyes focused forward, gripping the steering wheel, straining to see the ice covered road through the snow. He could picture his parents waiting at the hospital. As images of Mandy filled his mind, instinctively, he stepped on the gas. The girls screamed as the car began to slide. Woody hit the break as the car spun out of control. He remembered his dad telling him that if he ever slid on ice, don't step on the break. Too late. The car spun around and came to an abrupt halt as it slid into the back of the car in front of him. Stay calm. With the realization that his sister's tears were from fear, not injury, and with a wave from the driver in the car in front of him indicating that she was ok, albeit sitting in a car that was now stuck in a pile of snow, Woody braced himself for the cold that greeted him as he got out of the car. They had to get to the hospital but he couldn't leave this woman in her circumstance. "I'm so sorry," he said. "We've got to get to the hospital to see our sister." He continued relaying their story to the kind stranger. "I live just off the next exit." she said. "If you can give me a ride, my husband will take care of my car."

For a few moments, Woody forgot to pray. Prayer was as instinctive to him as breathing. How had he forgotten? With the kind stranger safely home and back on the road, his reflexes kicked in. When prayer is a reflex, peace follows. He reminded himself of this truth. In the middle of nowhere, on a snow covered road, driving in his first snow storm, Woody knew it was God who kept them safe. "Almost there," he announced to his sisters. He managed to grind the car through the unplowed side street and finally, into the emergency driveway. Ramming it into park, Woody sprinted with his sisters through the snow and into the emergency room doors.

Clarence paced the waiting area and occasionally, as far as he would dare, the small corridor leading to the closed doors of the ICU, stopping just short of the nurses' station that kept heavy guard over the closed doors. He paused long enough to squint his eyes, now focused on those doors. He turned away just in time to see Woody, Melody and Molly sprinting through the doors of the waiting room.

"What happened?", Melody immediately demanded to know. Clarence motioned for the kids to sit down. They agreed that they would not keep anything from the children. The battle for Mandy's life had always been one that the entire Green family fought together. Clarence reached for Beverly's hand and chose his words carefully. "Mandy coded," he said. We've been waiting for an update. No one is allowed to see Mandy right now until she is stable." "Pray louder," Beverly said. They all knew what she meant. There was nothing to do now, but wait, and pray.

5

A CRITICAL TIME

"For everything there is a season,
and a time for every purpose under heaven."

— ECCLESIASTES 3:1 (ASV)

Beverly glanced again at the clock on the wall above the corridor leading to the ICU. Either it wasn't working, or time was standing still. Clarence resumed his pacing. The kids were sprawled out on the floor. "This just isn't right." Beverly whispered to herself as she stood up from her seat. Melody watched as her mom marched directly down the corridor to the nurse's station. She had seen that determined look on her mother's face plenty of times over the years. She didn't need to hear what was being said. It was clear that her mom was fed up with waiting. After everything they had overcome with Mandy, Beverly wasn't going to spend hours in a waiting room without knowing the condition of her Mandy. This was not going to continue; not on Beverly's watch.

On cue, one of Mandy's doctors magically appeared from behind the guarded doors of the ICU and made his way toward the family. The doctor's kind eyes, now bloodshot from exhaustion, rested on Clarence, then Beverly and the children. He had come to know this family over the years and often referred to Mandy as his 'miracle patient'. If anyone had ever earned that title, it was little Mandy Green. "Mandy is stable," he said in his best 'be optimistic' doctor voice. He could tell Beverly wasn't buying it. "She's unresponsive right now but is breathing well with the help of a ventilator." Pausing briefly, he continued. "This is a critical time. There is no certainty of anything at the moment but we are doing our best to keep Mandy stable. You'll all be allowed back to see her soon." Doc knew Beverly all too well. "Beverly, come with me."

"Mandy is very swollen from the surgery." Clarence said, following the nurse down the corridor along with Woody, Melody and Molly. They had all witnessed Mandy in various stages of medical distress over the years, but Mandy's current condition was shocking. "Remember, even though it might seem like Mandy isn't responding to us, she can hear us." He was most worried about Melody. She and Mandy were so close. He and Beverly both understood what the doctor hadn't said. They were allowing them to see Mandy to say goodbye.

"A time for everything, a season and a right time for everything under heaven." Many have offered this passage from Ecclesiastes 3 as a comfort to those who are hurting. Usually, we only quote from the first verse and possibly throw in the 11th verse where God makes all things beautiful in His time, skipping over the difficult parts that clearly offer this truth - life is filled with uncertainties. In order to find comfort in this passage, we have to understand that even in the darkness, God is present. God is the Author of all things beautiful and everything in between. Matthew Henry said it beautifully, "To expect unchanging happiness in a changing world, must end in disappointment." We don't know what time it is, but we know that there is a time to give birth and a time to die. When we are going through difficulty, it is comforting to think of the pain ending. "A time to be born, and a time to die." But is it comforting to know that there is a time to die when someone you love is about to? We all understand Life's ebbs and flows. A crucial truth for all of us to understand is that "no moment is ever wasted in the unfolding of God's plan." Yet, how do you tell the Green family what purpose there would be in the death of their young child? The essence of faith is the trust in God's promise to protect his children. The Green's chose to rely on that word of God as they battled the dark forces surrounding them. Without an awareness of that promise, it would be difficult to persevere and impossible to withstand these soul-crushing trials.

6

ALL THINGS NEW

"Therefore, if anyone is in Christ, he is a new creation;
old things have passed away;
behold, all things have become new."

— 2 CORINTHIANS 5:17 (NKJV)

Clarence Green, at 8 years old, sat on the daybed on the other side of the room and with eyes of a child losing their innocence, looked across at his father just in time to see his dad rest his head back in his recliner. It was the last movement he ever saw from his father. Clarence remembers going to bed that night. It wasn't the usual bedtime prayer that he had been taught and routinely prayed, "Now I lay me down to sleep, I pray to the Lord my soul to keep. If I should die before I wake, I pray to the Lord my soul to take." That night, it was a different prayer that he prayed with the innocence of his young heart and with all the earnest desire that he held within his spirit. "Please God, bring my daddy back to me." The experience of seeing his daddy pass was so traumatic that he was physically sick to his stomach. Night after night, he would go to bed, anguished, and he would pray the same prayer, "Please, God, bring my daddy back." And many nights after he prayed, he would dream the same dream. He would see his daddy in his '47 Ford Coupe, only to wake and realize that the image was not real. But in the loneliness of the night, it was a beautiful glimpse of the past that God used to comfort a young boy's heart.

Clarence loved farm life. He was a handsome child with hazel eyes and thick dark blonde hair that he couldn't be bothered to comb. He was curious about everything. The endless supply of dairy cows, pigs, chickens, rabbits and other animals along with the crops his family grew were his greatest source of wonder and learning. He was a country boy, through and through. There was nothing he loved more than settling in for some good ol' fun with his siblings. Hunting, running through the hills and on this night, camping with his brother in those hills, brought the unexpected. They set up camp, gathered wood and settled in, just in time to shelter from an unannounced storm. The lightning was fierce. "I love a good storm," he thought. "So, why am I afraid?" He felt something deep within his heart that wasn't right. He looked at his brother, sleeping. "I wonder if he knows my secrets." "I'm sorry Daddy," Clarence said silently. "I know you wouldn't be proud of me. I've stolen from that little country store. I've told dirty stories and started cursing." "I know God's not proud of the things I've done since you've been gone." At the young age of 10, in the stillness of this night, Clarence felt the truth of what is spoken in *Romans 2:15: "They demonstrate that God's law is written in their hearts, for their own conscience and thoughts either accuse them or tell them they are doing right." (NLT)*

Beverly Green, at 6 years old, did her best to lay still. "What if I just take a quick peek?" she thought as her mother and father, along with their pastor and his wife, gathered around her bedside to pray. She was tired, extremely weak from her illness and had been bedridden for 2 weeks. Her mischievous, striking blue eyes were clouded with fever, hidden under the backdrop of her chestnut brown hair. Is this what Jesus meant when speaking of "2 or 3 gathered in His name?" In the middle of the prayer, she allowed herself a quick peek, but shut her eyes quickly. Would God heal her if her eyes were open as they prayed? She let herself fall deeper into prayer with the adults and strangely, felt God's presence too. When they said, 'Amen', she opened her eyes. Beverly had felt God's touch from her head to her toes. The unchanging, eternal love which compelled Jesus to heal Simon Peter's mother-in-law from a fever is recorded in *Luke 4:39*. *"And He stood over her, and rebuked the fever; and it left her: and immediately she arose and ministered unto them."* *(KJV)* This same love was present that day for Beverly. She knew who had healed her. God authored her story with this moment, and claimed her as one of His own.

Like Clarence, Beverly's father passed away in her youth. "I miss you, Dad." It still hurts so much." He was her true north, her constant. "There's nobody like you, Dad." She let the tears flow freely when alone. "God," she said, "maybe someday I could have a husband that would love my soul as much as my Dad did. " Someone who would not only love me, but would love my soul." Perhaps, Beverly thought, if she could truly know the God her father loved, she might discover the great love he had had for her.

We can do without a lot of things in this life. We can do without material comforts and entertainment. We can do without worldly knowledge and we can even do without money. But deep within us is the longing for our soul to be cared for. There has been, or there will come a day in all of our lives, when we understand that God is speaking directly to the heart of our spirit. God comforts as only a Heavenly Father can do - fully, wholly, tenderly and lovingly, wiping away the tears to restore our spirit. Beverly grew up attending church with her family each week, but she had not spent time searching for the truth in the good book. However, she knew this simple truth; she needed God. There is a beautiful old hymn, "Sun of My Soul", written by John Keble. "Sun of my soul, thou Savior dear, it is not night if thou be near." Jesus is the Sun in our Soul. It can be a dark world indeed when we believe there is no one who cares for our soul.

Beverly's search came to an end one day in October of 1967, as a young woman. "It's like this song is being sung just for me, directly from heaven." "I understand now, Dad. I know how you loved me, how you loved God and mom and our family." When you taught me to "Love the Lord your God with all your mind and with all your strength," it was because that's where your supply of love came from. It's the same love that healed me when I was 6 and the same love that is rising within me right now. "I wish you were here so I could say thank you, Dad." "It will be well, Beverly." Her father's voice echoed in her spirit with the words he had spoken so many times. She felt his spirit, without a doubt, at this life changing moment.

God loves a simple faith that is as a child's. Children believe. Simple faith is faith which is uncomplicated by "grown up" thoughts, ambitions and fears; it simply believes and solely trusts that God is who He says He is, and that He will do what He has said He will do. *In Luke 10:21 we read "At that same time Jesus was filled with the joy of the Holy Spirit, and he said, "O Father, Lord of heaven and earth, thank you for hiding these things from those who think themselves wise and clever, and for revealing them to the childlike." (NLT)*

Clarence experienced this the next Sunday in church when God spoke to the heart of this young, ten-year-old child. " "I'm so sorry for stealing and for the wrong I've done. What a list I have for just a little guy!" A young man came and sat beside him. He said,

"Clarence, if you'll just tell God - just put it all together in a big basket." Clarence asked God to forgive him. There was an immediate peace within his heart which he had never felt before. "The joy bells of Heaven are ringing down in my soul. I've never been so happy in all my life!", he exclaimed. How do we thank an everlasting, eternal God for the very salvation of our souls? There is nothing we can do to earn it. We can never repay the cost, the price is too high yet, when we love someone, we desire to please them. Clarence and Beverly, in their youth, desired to please God. They didn't seek material blessings or physical riches of this world. They sought the blessing and richness of God's love that took root in the very depths of their souls, and the peace that came from the assurance of a love that is secure and unwavering.

Clarence admitted later in life that he was not a very patient man and it was one of the things he had difficulty with in his younger years. He desired a soulmate to be his lifelong companion. He was committed to waiting as God had told him. But, "He didn't leave me hanging very long," he says. "And the girl I met coming across the church grounds who had shared that wonderful bible verse with me, was to be the one. She told me, as written by John, "If all the great works of Jesus had been written, they would fill volumes (of books) the world could not contain." She was to be my bride - my "Bevie". Later in life, Clarence said, "You probably can understand that, after how long it takes me to tell my little story, and the whole book of items that the Lord has done for me - you can see how many volumes (about Jesus) there would be if we stacked all of them up." That very moment was written by God when the world began.

Patience is a virtue, it is often said. As with most things that we wait and hope for, the end is better than the beginning. Should we really wait when there are opportunities for immediate satisfaction and instant gratification at every turn? In our modern world of fast paced technology, which gives instant access to information along with the ability to quickly satisfy our wants, needs and desires, the idea of waiting on God might seem foreign and "old fashioned." *"Since ancient times no one has heard, no ear has perceived, no eye has seen any God besides you, who acts on behalf of those who wait for Him." (Isaiah 64:4 NIV1984)* Yes, we wait on God. His plan is always more sufficient, more desirable and more perfect than what we may accomplish with our own strength or in the satisfying of our temporary desires.

7

JOY AND HEARTACHE

Psalm 9:1-2 "I will praise you, O LORD, with all my heart;
I will tell of all your wonders.
I will be glad and rejoice in you;
I will sing praise to your name, O Most High."

— NIV1984

Beverly and Clarence looked forward with excitement to the time when they would begin their family together. They began to pray that God would bless them with a child. God answered their prayers and they rejoiced when, in March of 1972, Walter was born, filling their home with the joyful sounds of a newborn. They loved being parents and, as Walter grew from a baby into a playful toddler, they both knew they wanted more children. But, Beverly suffered a miscarriage during her second pregnancy. It tore their hearts open. For the first time, Beverly experienced the same grief as her own mother had, when losing her baby brother. Yet, in February of 1974, God blessed this young couple with another little boy, Wayne. With two new arrivals, their family was growing quickly and they knew they needed more living space. The Greens moved into their new home only months before Beverly gave birth to their third son, Woody, in October of 1975. Beverly had prayed for a girl with this pregnancy, but God gently answered, "No, next time." They were over the moon with excitement and settled nicely into their home when God answered Beverly's prayer for a little girl. Melody was born in April of 1977 and quickly became the center of her brothers' attention.

This was the fulfillment of their dreams. They both devoted all their energy to raising a family in an atmosphere of total love and spiritual awareness. Yet, they suffered, like many young couples, through the expected hardships of raising a family. Four children required time and devotion. Children went to see the doctor when ill, to school to learn, and prayed to the Lord as their mother and father taught them. Their budget left no room for frivolous spending, yet they gratefully received God's continual and abundant provision for their family's every need. With four children between the ages of 4 and 9, Beverly had her hands full and was immersed in keeping things orderly at home. Regarding the subject of family prayer, Beverly would not negotiate. It would be only under the most challenging of circumstances that the children would be given an exemption from family devotion time. Family prayer meant that every family member was present. Clarence, Beverly, Walter, Wayne, Woody and Melody. This was a most treasured part of Beverly's day. She asked that her children pray aloud and from the youngest to the oldest, they each would take their turn. Beverly loved hearing the prayers of her children. Clarence made the Bible stories and scripture come alive with his flair for storytelling. Their family prayers became the threads which, when woven together, created the tapestry of their faith.

God was included in every activity, meal, conversation - always as near as their next breath.

Mandy was born August 17, 1981, a healthy, beautiful child. The answer to Woody's prayer. Her red hair and bright blue eyes went perfectly with her vivacious personality. The first year of Mandy's life was filled with the milestones that fill parents' hearts with joy. A first cry, a first smile, a first kiss, a first giggle; the first reaction of delight when being tickled and, in Mandy's life, the first time she reached out to hold her big sister's hand. With three boys and two girls, the Green household was active and busy and as she grew, Mandy added to the fun and happiness in their small home in Newark, Ohio. Although the boys still outnumbered the girls, the girls were catching up quickly. There is nothing quite like the joy of watching your child take their first steps. Joy is followed by the surprising realization that she has just taken her first steps toward a life independent of you. They are, in fact, separate from you. Although the bonds that tie our children to us are as delicate as silk, they also remain strong as iron. They may bend, but will never be broken.

How we mothers love! Each tear our children cry is lovingly wiped away and etched upon a mother's heart. We bear their sorrow with them and if we could, we would bear their sorrow for them. We see this very same bond with Mary and Jesus, from his young days through his crucifixion. Through these relationships, we are given a glimpse of the love our Heavenly Father has for His children. Jesus said, "Bring your burdens to Me." *Psalm 68:19 "Praise be to the Lord, to God our Savior, who daily bears our burdens. Selah" (NIV1984).* As we cast our cares down at the foot of the cross, Christ is faithful to pick them up. We try our best. Laying down our burdens, our cares and worries, the hurt and pain, and even with the invitation from our great God, we struggle to let go of it all. In our own strength, we are not able. *"Take my yoke"*, Jesus says in *Matthew 11:30 "For My yoke is easy and My burden is light."(KJV)* The intention was never for us to walk through this world alone. Yet, as much as we love our children, God loves them more. We are His, and they are His and we exist under His love and protection. Every precious moment with Mandy was captured in Beverly's heart, to hold in remembrance, and to store for her strength to confront what would follow. No one but God knew what was waiting for this faithful mother and her family.

8

THE WOLF AT THE DOOR

"For the LORD *God is a sun and shield:*
the LORD *will give grace and glory:*
no good thing will He withhold from them that walk uprightly.
O LORD *of hosts, blessed is the man who trusts in you."*

— PSALM 84:11-12 NKJV

The Green family had just finished blowing out the candles on Mandy's first birthday cake when, in September of 1982, Beverly and Clarence found themselves sitting across from a doctor. This man was doing his best to explain why Mandy wasn't recovering from a simple ear infection. This medical mystery sent doctors on a lengthy evaluation process which included the testing of Mandy's blood. "What's Histiocytosis X?" Beverly asked, trying to make sense of the scary medical terms and the name of a disease that would jeopardize the life of her precious child. "It's an incredibly rare blood disease - a rare form of leukemia," the doctor said. He told them that there had only been a few cases ever recorded in the

United States - 25 to be exact. The amount of data available on this disease was almost non-existent, except for one statistic - the survival rate. It was statistically, one in one million. There was silence. The doctor tried again, clearing his throat. "It's a disease of the blood involving an increased number of immune cells called histiocytes. Everyone has histiocytes; they cleanse our blood and keep it free from infection." Silence again. He continued, "Simply put, Histiocytosis X occurs when there are abnormal amounts of histiocytes in the body that move into tissues where they are not normally found. Instead of providing protection to the body by fighting infection, they take up residence where they don't belong and begin attacking the organs and tissue where they reside." "Kind of like a terrorist." Clearing his throat, the good Doctor continued. "Some forms of Histiocytosis are specific to certain organs of the body, Mandy's type, 'Histiocytosis X', is affecting her entire body."

"How do you know with certainty this is the disease Mandy has?" Beverly wanted to know. "What does this mean for our daughter? Our future children? What is the treatment?" The doctor looked at Beverly and Clarence, wishing he could offer clear and hopeful answers to her questions. "There is no known cure." Silence. "Do you have any other questions?" Clarence shook his head. The questions he had would not be answered on this day, or in the near future.

They had no idea how life changing this diagnosis would be for their family, but Beverly and Clarence agreed that shielding the other children from the truth was not an option. Whatever trials would come, they would face them together, as a family. Beverly heard God's voice clearly. "If you walk upright, morning, noon, day and night, I'll be there." It was as if God perched an angel on her shoulder that kept singing that song. She entrusted God to be her sun and her shield, her light and her protector, giving His grace and glory to this stunning news. Deep in her heart, she firmly believed He would not fail them. He would be there for them and see them through it all. Many times in the coming years, Beverly would recall God's promise to renew her hope and strength. As for this particular day, September 27, 1982, the Green family had done all that they could do as Mandy received her first blood transfusion designed to battle this rare condition. The doctors finally released Mandy from the hospital, and the Greens were able to return to home as a family. They were exhausted, hungry and had no idea what the next day might bring.

Mandy's disease immediately began its relentless attack on her small body. The progression was frighteningly rapid, causing what looked like moth-eaten holes in her bones that would allow her blood to escape through. Mandy would eventually bleed through her skeleton and skin, from her head to her toes. In the short time span of 10 months, her spleen enlarged to eleven times its normal size. Mandy's parents sat across from her doctor and listened in disbelief. How was that even possible? Beverly couldn't help but to recall the healthy nature of her other children at Mandy's age. They were continually on the move, laughing, running and playing until they grew tired, sweaty and content. Their activity may have paused for napping, sleeping and if she was lucky, eating. Mandy was unable to sit upright. She couldn't balance herself because her spleen was so much larger than it should have been for her little body. Then, another bombshell dropped. Mandy required surgery to remove her enlarged spleen. There are very real risks associated with any "normal" surgery, but Mandy's circumstances were anything but normal. If her parents decided that they did not want their little girl to undergo such an invasive procedure, there was a good possibility that the spleen would continue growing and Mandy's illness would quickly progress, ending her life. Clarence and Beverly were heartbroken to be faced with these options.

Should they risk their daughter's life for this surgery? The doctors' informed the parents that if the surgery was successful, her progress toward a recovery was still totally unknown.

In the final analysis, there was only one choice. Trust. Beverly trusted that God would keep the promise He had made to her. She trusted that He would see them through. She trusted that as much as she loved Mandy, God loved her daughter that much more. She was clinging to the words God gave her in song: "If you walk upright, morning, noon, day and night, I'll be there." Clarence and Beverly prayed. Their children prayed. Extended family prayed. Church family prayed. They invited God to protect Mandy during her surgery and guide the hands of the surgeons.

Beverly sat in the recovery room with one hand holding Mandy's, the other cradling her belly that was carrying their 6th child. Seeing her tiny daughter - feeding tube in place and swollen almost beyond recognition, shocked her. She closed her eyes in prayer and praise for a moment, but quickly opened them again, blinking back tears. She searched her daughter's face for signs of pain, but Mandy seemed to be sleeping peacefully. Clarence sat with the remainder of his young family in the lobby as they waited for Mandy to be moved from recovery. The doctor explained to the children what they could expect to see. They would be allowed to see their sister one at a time. Melody, now 6 years old, heard the warning. "OK, when you go in there, she's going to have a feeding tube and she looks very swollen and bloated." All Melody ever dreamed of was having a baby sister to play dolls with. She wanted to be with her sister so they could play again. Melody paused at the door of the hospital room to have a peek before going in. She saw her mother sitting by Mandy, but could barely see Mandy in the hospital bed. As she nudged closer, she could see the feeding tube. Melody saw the swelling that she had been warned about. But, there are no words that could properly explain her sister's grave medical condition to Melody. There was no experience that Melody had ever had in her young life that could have prepared her as she looked at Mandy laying there in such a condition. She cautiously approached her mother and climbed up into the small amount of lap that was available between Beverly's pregnant belly and legs. She reached out to hold her sister's hand as she had done so many times before. She patted Mandy's hand as she had watched her mother do. "It's going to be ok, Mandy." "I prayed for you."

Life is not easy. We will experience sorrow, as all of us can testify. However, there is always the abiding peace of God's presence throughout our journey. God's promise to be with Beverly was enough to assure her of His presence. Now, exhausted and feeling very pregnant, Beverly returned home from the hospital to quickly gather clean clothes for her return. She went into her bedroom, quietly closed the door, sat down on her bed and cried. She didn't want the other children to see their mother crying, but she couldn't stop the tears that flowed from her spirit that was broken from the trauma of the day. She inhaled deeply, held it for a moment, then let go. She couldn't cry anymore. It was time for her to return to the hospital. God had spoken clearly to Beverly, through the pain of her broken heart. "I never promised you a bed of roses, but I did promise to be the Lily in your valley."

9

52 MINUTES

"Do not be afraid or discouraged,
for the Lord will personally go ahead of you.
He will be with you; he will neither fail you nor abandon you."

— DEUTERONOMY 31:8 NLT

"Grab a rake," Walter said. The sound of leaves crunching continued as the children worked together to create a great pile to jump into. More leaves escaped into the breeze than made it into Walter's pile, but it made for a fun game with his cousins and younger siblings as they waited for his Mom and Aunt Becky to finish preparing lunch. Every once in a while, the perfect fall day shows up in southern Ohio and on this one, Walter was determined to enjoy every moment of it.

His mom's voice urgently broke through their games. "Walter, get the car ready!" Walter immediately dropped the rake and sprinted to start the car. Glancing at his watch, he waited by the car, at the ready. His mom quickly swooped Mandy up and ran toward him.

He closed the passenger door behind her as she settled into the front seat with Mandy. The tell tale sign of blood dripping from his little sister's nose began, as it always did, without warning. Aunt Becky gave orders to Uncle Roger and Grandma to watch over the other children as she slid behind the wheel to drive while Walter simultaneously hopped into the back seat. They were off to the hospital. The clock was ticking. The Columbus Childrens' Hospital was exactly 52 minutes away. Speed was critical. Walter glanced at his watch again.

"Need more diapers, Walter." Beverly struggled to keep up with the blood, now flowing freely from Mandy's nose and mouth. Walter traded his mom a clean, cloth diaper for a bloody one and added it to the others in the bucket next to him. He wondered what was worse, the bleeding or the sound of Mandy choking on the large clots of blood her little body struggled to discharge. With every minute that went by, more of Mandy's blood was lost. They could only watch as life drained out of her precious body. Beverly cried out and begged God. "Please help her!" For one moment, the chaos quieted. She looked into Mandy's bright blue eyes, now overshadowed by shock and trauma. Mandy's hand brushed her mother's face as Beverly held her tightly. That quiet moment was short lived. In a flash, her little girl's eyes began to roll back into her skull. Beverly could only see the white of her eyes, the blue sparkles having disappeared. "Mandy, talk to Mother! God, please, help her!"

Beverly, Aunt Becky and Walter shared the same unspoken thought. "We're not going to make it." They were 30 minutes into their drive and time was running out. Aunt Becky saw the Pataskala Fire House and made the last minute decision to turn into the driveway. She laid on the horn to alert them, stopping the car directly next to the parked ambulance. The paramedics took one look into the car, saw Mandy and Beverly covered in blood and immediately motioned to get the ambulance ready. "She is three years old." Beverly answered their questions as they calmly, yet quickly transferred her and Mandy into the ambulance, launched the sirens and sped off to the Children's Hospital in Columbus.

Walter sat quietly in the back seat as Aunt Becky followed behind the ambulance. He stared at the bucket next to him, then to the front of the car where his mother and Mandy had been and finally down to his own hands. "Mandy's blood," he thought. Through the eyes of a 12 year old child, he watched the ambulance drive off with his mom and baby sister. "Mom was undone by this one." There was so much blood. He was well aware of the timeline and looking again at his watch, began ticking off minutes in his mind - 30 minutes of driving - about 7 minutes to load into the ambulance - and they still had almost 20 minutes to go. It was always the same race against the clock. He never felt relief until they pulled into the hospital driveway, knowing the nurses would immediately take over as soon as they saw Mandy and the "watch over her life" would be transferred to the professionals. As Aunt Becky made the final turn onto the hospital emergency road, young Walter breathed a sigh of relief, unaware that he had been holding his breath.

They made it on time that day. The mission was to repeat this, every time, without fail, two to three times a week, for the next three years. Failure was not an option.

10

FLEETING THOUGHTS

Psalm 9:1-2 "I will praise you, O LORD, with all my heart;
I will tell of all your wonders.
I will be glad and rejoice in you;
I will sing praise to your name, O Most High."

— NIV1984

"This one was close." Clarence took one last look into the overnight bag to be sure he hadn't forgotten anything Beverly requested. He walked by Mandy's beloved stuffed bear and paused. "Wanna go see Mandy?" Arms full, Clarence grabbed the bear, tossed everything into his truck and walked around to the driver's side, stopping for a moment to take in the landscape of their little house. "It's perfect." Beverly had said when she first saw the house. Clarence agreed. It wasn't luxurious and it wasn't big. It wasn't worth a whole lot of money, but it was rich in memories and reminded him of his growing years in Adamsville, Ohio, on his parent's farm.

Clarence pulled onto the highway, lost in thoughts of simpler days gone by and life on the farm. This was often his way of dealing with the rush of judgments his mind would have to make, and the pressure that came along with those judgments. "Wish I could hear your voice right now, Dad." "All I've ever wanted was to be the father and husband you would be proud of." Tears burned his eyes. "Well, how am I doin' Dad?" The image of his young father sitting in his recliner, laying his head back for the final time, was seared into his mind. "Please God, bring my Daddy back." Night after night, Clarence prayed the same prayer, and the same dream would come to comfort him. He'd see his father driving his '47 Ford Coupe. He knew God heard his request. A grin replaced his tears. Wow, he had almost forgotten about that car.

"It's love. It's love. I know it's wonderful love!" Clarence found himself singing while he drove, as he would often do when he and his Bevie were courting. He chuckled. As a young man, his faith was filled with passion and fire. He desired to find a soul mate, a companion to share his life with, who had that same passion. He unsuccessfully pursued many relationships. He was pushing too hard. Finally, he asked God to pick out "his girl." And, walking across the church grounds, one bright day, came Beverly, looking for a ride home. God's universe had the two talking and Bevie shared her favorite Bible verse with him. What a treasure God brought to him. "I hit it big time!" Clarence continued his impromptu singing while driving. It took a bit of convincing that day, fourteen years ago, for Beverly to allow him to give her a ride home. "I insist." "Well..." she said. "I do need a ride." She looked him square in the eye. "You can just leave me off at the curb." That did it. He was hooked. He vowed his life and love to Bevie seven months later, on the same day his father married his mother so many years ago. "We've got God and we've got each other." What more could a man desire?

Clarence shifted his gaze to the bear he had given to Mandy on her first birthday, now sitting next to him in the passenger seat. He hadn't realized how big it was in the toy store. Clarence thought the bear's mischievous grin was a perfect match for Mandy's personality. "Goodness, Clarence!" Beverly said when he first brought it home, watching him struggle to get it inside their small doorway. "She'll grow into it," Clarence said. He was still waiting for Mandy to catch up with that bear. He breathed in deeply and held it for a moment before releasing, choking back the tears, remembering Mandy's laugh as she held out her arms when he gave her the bear. "Dear God, I'm a mess."

"We're not super young," Beverly had told him when they began their family. "Well, I feel old now, Bevie. Much older than 36 years." Feels like Walter was just born, and here he is 12 years old. But, it was Woody who had the inspired notion of praying for Melody to have a baby sister. "That one is a prayer warrior, like his Mom." "What are you whispering, Woody?" Beverly had asked Woody during family prayer. He replied, "Well, I am praying for Melody to have a baby sister." Woody reasoned that Melody would benefit from having a younger sister. Plus, he determined, if he could just outsource his doll playing duties with Melody to another sister, that would take care of things without hurting Melody's feelings. Clarence smiled. "The faith of a child." Melody was completely smitten with her younger sister. She had her own real-life doll to play with. Clarence reached over to pat the head of the bear. "We've been through it, friend." "Am I talking to stuffed bears now?" He rolled the window down further. Maybe the crisp, fall air would help to clear his head. Life before the battle. He could hardly remember it. It may as well have been 10 years instead of 2. All these fleeting thoughts and more continued to run through his mind, as he drove at a record pace to the Hospital Emergency Room's doors. There, he would let his child off at the curb, just as he did with his beloved wife, all those years ago.

THE NEW NORMAL

"When you pass through the deep, stormy sea,
you can count on me to be there with you.
When you pass through raging rivers,
You will not drown.
When you walk through persecution like fiery flames,
you will not be burned;
the flames will not harm you."

— ISAIAH 43:2 TPT

During the first two years of Mandy's illness, Beverly spent most of her days at Children's Hospital, in Columbus, Ohio. During those early times, it was a constant back and forth between the hospital and home. When they were able to make the trip home, there was no certainty of how long the family would be together. Oftentimes, their stay at home was cut short. It might be a matter of only a few hours before Mandy would begin to bleed, and their urgent 52 minute trek back to Children's Hospital would begin again. There was never the assurance that any day would be "normal". There was never a guarantee that their family dinner would not be interrupted by a trip to the hospital. To live each day with such clear uncertainty serves to magnify this truth; we are powerless in the face of many circumstances that come into our lives. Each peaceful day is a gift not to be taken for granted. In Mandy's case, the doctors offered no hope that tomorrow would be different. There was no promise of a cure for this disease, only their best guess as to what might prolong Mandy's life. Through this time of trouble and uncertainty, one thing remained clear: Keep Mandy alive at all costs.

Yet, in the midst of all the uncertainty, Beverly and Clarence made a commitment to each other and to their children. "As much as it is possible to do so, we are going to live normal lives." "We are going to do our best to create fun, adventure and enjoy time together as a family." Sunday gatherings provided the simplest of pleasures and these moments became the greatest of treasure to them. Clarence was determined that his family would not surrender to a life spent within the confines of their home. One by one, he was able to purchase bicycles for the entire family so that they could enjoy bike rides together. Clarence carried Mandy in a seat on the back of his bike and Molly, the youngest of the children, rode on the back of Beverly's bike. The older children loved the freedom of pedaling on their own. They would strap the bikes onto the roof and into the back of whichever of their two station wagons happened to be running at the time, and drive to one of their favorite places of adventure near the Blackhand Gorge River in Toboso, Ohio. The rock walls that had been cut-through along a former railway added a touch of mystery and created a pathway that took these "bikers" to quarries, rivers, cliffs and waterfalls. The children created secret, fantastic stories of their adventures that would be fondly remembered and laughed over during a family bonfire. The children, in particular, enjoyed watching other people paddling down the rough river, in their canoes, making their way down the mysterious river. Some days they would pack a picnic. On special days, they would celebrate with a treat from Dairy Queen and bring their lunch home after riding the trails.

There was always the fear and risk of exposing Mandy to other illnesses. Clarence and Beverly discovered that the time between lunch and dinner was a quiet time in their local restaurants. Mandy could be around people at a distance. When attending church, they were careful to arrive late, leave early and sit far from the crowd. An innocent hug from someone who might be carrying a cold or flu could have grave consequences for their Mandy. The entire family became used to this type of self-isolation. Although these dinners, bike rides and outings were precious moments in their lives, the family knew that at any moment on any given day, everything could change. The fun and simple pleasures they worked hard to create and maintain were not a given - all of it would and did stop the instant Mandy would begin to bleed. On many occasions, play time was interrupted or eliminated completely. Family meals were fair game, too, and were often put on hold - to be continued - or cancelled for that day.

The process of receiving blood transfusions through an I.V. became the required treatment ritual that would sustain Mandy's life. One cubic millimeter of human blood contains 5 million oxygen carrying red blood cells, approximately 5,000 to 10,000 different types of white blood cells that fight off infection and 200,000 to 300,000 platelets which aid in blood clotting. There is no artificial substitute for human blood. Reflecting on the magnitude of a 'simple cell', we can only contemplate the complexity and miracle of creation. And we can say along with the psalmist in *Psalm 139:14, "I will praise You, for I am fearfully and wonderfully made; marvelous are Your works, And that my soul knows very well " (NKJV)* The

Greens were faced with the possibility of losing their daughter daily - for 4 ½ years. Daily, her survival depended on life sustaining blood. God's word is clear that blood is the lifeline of every living creature. It flows through us and sustains us. It is also blood that redeems us. In *Ephesians 2:13-14a, God's word is clear: "But now you have been united with Christ Jesus. Once you were far away from God, but now you have been brought near to Him through the blood of Christ. For Christ Himself has brought peace to us." (NLT)* I wonder how many drops of blood were shed by Christ for all of us. His blood, His very life, was shed for us and freely given. We serve an awesome God.

MIRACLE CHILD

See from His head, His hands, His feet,
Sorrow and love flow mingled down!
Did e'er such love and sorrow meet,
Or thorns compose so rich a crown?
Were the whole realm of nature mine,
That were a present far too small;
Love so amazing, so divine,
Demands my soul, my life, my all.

— ISAAC WATTS - 1719

L ove, joy and sorrow. Beverly felt all of them in the deepest places of her soul. Joy mingled with sorrow. Fear mingled with faith. Doubt, clinging desperately to hope. A contradiction of emotions emerged that can only be understood through the lens of everlasting and ever present grace.

Have you ever felt so overwhelmed by the emotional weight of worry, stress, anxiety, and fear that you physically crumbled? Have you been trapped beneath burdens that weighed so heavily on your mind and spirit that you felt there was no way of escape? There are days, moments maybe, that offer a welcome, but brief distraction, yet are void of any promise of long lasting relief from your pain. All too soon, that familiar feeling returns and rises to crush your spirit and your battle for peace begins again. We cry out to our God, as we again lay our burdens down upon his shoulders, to live through the day. There is nowhere else that we can turn. Daily, and moment by moment, we rely on our Lord to give us rest, guidance and strength. Cry out and seek him. Only in His arms will we find rest for the weary and burdened, strength for the faint hearted, and peace for a broken spirit. These are the fruits of faith.

Beverly sat in the living room rocking chair, pillow on her lap, Mandy on top of the pillow, hoping the soothing rhythm would lull her to sleep. In the middle of the night, with no one around to hear her, she entrusted God with her most private thoughts. "I'm exhausted. Weary in my bones." she told Him. She placed one hand on her belly. "I know these thoughts are not from you. I am excited about this new baby, but inwardly I wonder if I have the strength." "You do." she heard God say. "Nights and days are becoming blurred together, between the hospital and home." She comforted herself by singing one of her favorite hymns to Mandy who was staring up at her. "How is this child still awake?" It had been such a long day. I wonder if we'll be sleeping at all tonight. "There is no certainty, God." Softly, she began to sing as Mandy continued to look at her, expectant and curious.

> *"I have found a friend in Jesus- He's everything to me,*
> *He's the fairest of ten thousand to my soul;*
> *The Lily of the Valley- in Him alone I see*
> *All I need to cleanse and make me fully whole.*
> *In sorrow He's my comfort, in trouble He's my stay,*

He tells me ev'ry care on Him to roll;
He's the Lily of the Valley, the Bright and Morning Star,
He's the greatest of ten thousand to my soul.

— CHARLES W. FRY 1881

Her soft singing reassured her. "No matter how deep the valley, I know God resides within me." Mandy wouldn't speak, but when Beverly finished singing, she reached up to touch her mother's cheek as if to say, "Mommy, sing it again." Again and again Beverly sang, but inwardly, her heart still felt as though it had been broken in two. She prayed as she held her precious child. Every tear Mandy cried was etched upon her mother's heart; she bore the burden of sorrow along with Mandy - and if it were possible, she would have taken it from her. "Cast our cares," Beverly thought, "and at the foot of the cross, Jesus is faithful to pick them up."

She looked down at Mandy. "You survived that surgery, Mandy. God has given you a spirit of bold courage and fighting determination. The doctors call you their 'miracle child'." Mandy smiled. "You're going to be a big sister." Beverly felt peace fill her spirit, overcoming her lingering fears. Mandy closed her eyes with Beverly and just like that, they were both asleep. The battle would now have to wait until the next morning.

13

OUT OF DARKNESS

"Weeping may endure for a night,
but joy cometh in the morning."

— PSALM 30:5B KJV

"The baby is lodged in the birth canal." The doctor quickly gave orders as Clarence watched, helpless, while nurses hurried past him to prepare a surgical room for an emergency cesarean. "Please, Lord, don't take them from me." Clarence prayed. Beverly was exhausted, physically and emotionally, before her labor began. "Mother and child are both in distress. Their heart rates are dropping. Let's move!" The doctor rushed past Clarence. Then, a quick pause. "It's going to be ok," he said, and continued to run down the hallway. Clarence ran the other way to use the phone. "Pastor, pray!" he said when Pastor Wilson answered. "I can't lose my wife. I can't lose my child." "God keeps His promises, Clarence. We will pray." In silent prayer, Clarence sobbed with his head in his hands. "God, you promised you would be there for us. I can't lose my Bevie. We're on this roller coaster of life together. This child is a special gift. Oh, Lord save them both."

"What's taking so long?" Pacing the hallway wasn't helping, but he couldn't sit still. He turned to pace in the other direction and almost ran into the doctor. Clarence looked at him, afraid to ask either question. The doctor smiled. "You have a beautiful daughter," he said. "Beverly is stable." "Thank you, Lord," was all Clarence managed to choke out. And then, "A daughter!"

On August 22nd, 1983, the Greens welcomed their sixth child and third little girl, Molly, into their family. Beverly lay in the hospital bed with Molly. Clarence wanted to surprise Beverly. "I'll bring her back immediately," he had said to the nurses at Children's Hospital. It was all worth it just to see Beverly's face light up with surprise when he walked into her room carrying Mandy. "Come on up, Mandy." she said, patting the hospital bed next to her. Mandy appeared excited to see her new baby sister. Clarence gently placed Mandy onto the bed, followed by Melody who climbed up. "Well, I don't think my heart could get much more full of God's goodness." Beverly said. "I guess there's no room on that hospital bed for Dad," Clarence teased. Clarence bent to give all of his girls a kiss and held tightly onto Beverly's hand.

Later, Clarence and Beverly sat in quiet conversation in the hospital room, planning for Beverly and Molly to go home. Mandy was still in the hospital. "I'll stay with Mandy." Clarence said. "You'll need time to recover at home with Molly." Beverly's doctor hesitated outside her room. "I'm sorry to interrupt your conversation," he said. He knew what this family was going through. "No need to apologize." Clarence said, standing to shake his hand. "Thank you for everything you've done for my girls." Beverly looked at him expectantly for instructions to go home, although she sensed something was not right. "I'm sorry," he said.

"We can't let Molly go home yet. I listened to Molly's heart when she was born; something doesn't sound right. I decided to take some x-rays and conduct a few other tests." "I need to do more testing to be safe before I release her." "There's just no way something can be wrong with another little baby," Beverly pleaded as the familiar arrow of fear pierced her heart. "Thank you, Doctor," was all Clarence could manage to say as he sat next to Beverly again. "I'll have more answers later today or tomorrow." Clarence took Beverly's hand. She shook her head. "There is just no way this can be happening." "Let's try to get some rest, Bevie." "We'll know more soon." He was worried about Beverly's recovery. "I'll be right here. Get some rest." They both shared the same unspoken thoughts. More time in the hospital. More tests. More fears, more tears, more uncertainty and doubt. More prayers.

"There is nothing that needs to be done - nothing that can be done at this moment." The doctor informed them as he held the test results in his hand. "Molly's pulmonary valve is too thick. Essentially, it is obstructing the flow of blood to the right ventricle, and ultimately, to her lungs. She'll need to be monitored very closely for the first month, but she can go home. If there is no improvement, she'll have to undergo open heart surgery."

Anchored into Beverly's soul was the moment God had authored in her own life long ago - the moment that His great love had reached down to heal her as a young girl. Now, it was their daughter, Molly, for whom they prayed. Once home, Clarence and Beverly linked arms together with Pastor Wilson and his wife. They all prayed together as they held Molly in that little circle. They prayed, and God answered.

When it seems like we are lost at every turn, and nothing good can be seen coming to our aid, eyes of faith see hope. Eyes of faith see, with assurance, into the mind of God. God's Word says that if we have faith as small as a mustard seed, we can move a mountain. We begin our climb out of darkness. We stumble. We fall. We get knocked down. But even the smallest measure of faith can give us the strength to get back up on our feet and press on. We continue our journey through tribulations of fear, betrayal, and hopelessness, but are called to see beyond the clouds that darken our vision. "To see the light of hope when nothing seems possible." *Matthew 17:20a: "Truly I tell you, if you have faith as small as a mustard seed, you can say to this mountain, 'Move from here to there,' and it will move. Nothing will be impossible for you."* (NIV) It is prayer that moves the hand of God. And the tiniest of faith which moves mountains.

God answered the circle of prayers that continued beyond that day. A month later, the doctor was able to give good news to Clarence and Bevie. "Molly is doing just fine. Surgery won't be necessary. Just continue monitoring her." Our foundation of faith is built upon trust in the Lord and His word. Throughout their season of trials and tribulations, the Green family relied upon this word each and every day. Their faith is a living testament of this unchanging truth and the essence of their hope.

STANDIN' IN THE FIRE

"It is of the Lord's mercies that we are not consumed, because his compassions fail not."

— LAMENTATIONS 3:22 KJV

Clarence was thankful to be leaving the work site. It had been a long, hot and difficult day, but he was thankful for the work. His body was tired, but his mind raced relentlessly. Thoughts of his family, work, bills, mortgage payments, past due taxes and hospital expenses consumed him. He had been living at the hospital with Mandy for almost six weeks, racing home after work for only a few minutes here and there. Often he would only have a short time to stop home, grab clean clothes as needed, kiss his wife and children, including their new baby girl Molly and maybe have a bite to eat. Then, it was the 52 minute dash. Those were the good days. Most days, however, he left work, rushed to the nearest fast food drive through and continued directly to the hospital. *"How long will you forget me, Lord? Forever? How long will you look the other way when I am in need?"*

Clarence prayed just as the writer of Psalms did so long ago. *"How long must I be hiding daily anguish in my heart? How long shall my enemy have the upper hand? Answer me, O Lord my God; give me light in my darkness lest I die." (Psalm 13:1-3 TLB)* "My thoughts - my very life are consumed with worry, grief and helplessness. Joy eludes me." Clarence continued his prayer, speaking his own psalm out loud. "I'm tryin' to hold onto the promise you gave to my Bevie. You promised to see us through. But how? And, when?" He struggled with these ever present thoughts. His heart could not see past the overwhelming evidence. "We are losing the battle." Nothing in his circumstance moved to give sight to his faith in "the promise."

He spent that evening holding Mandy, softly singing hymns to her while rocking her to sleep. But, once Mandy fell into a deep sleep, he felt isolated and alone again. Some nights, unable to fall asleep, he would fight against the tears. Other nights, he was unable to stop his tears that flowed from the exhaustion, pain and roller coaster of emotions which he fought to keep under control all day long. On this night, Clarence laid on the cot and couldn't stop the dark thoughts running through his head. He wept. "I am utterly powerless in my efforts. Lord, this ain't fair, you know. I wanted to preach. I wanted to help other people. And, Lord, just look at my world caving in!" There were many low periods in the battle for Mandy's life. For Clarence, this was one of them. He had grown accustomed to seeing his little daughter hooked up to the blood supplies and medicines. Trapped between a place of gratitude for the medicines which kept Mandy alive and anger and disdain for their necessity, his anguish deepened. "The bills are impossible, Lord. I am ashamed. I am powerless."

Beverly and Clarence always chose to pay the hospital bills first, even if it meant living on little or no money, relying on church donations from friends for the daily needs of their entire family. They were falling behind on their mortgage. The IRS continued their relentless pursuit for tax payments. In the darkness of this time, in the battle that was waged in their circumstance, a larger war was being fought within him. While driving one night, a dark, ominous voice rose within him and came forward. "Why don't you just hook it to the right and catch a pole? Your family will be better off without you." Sleep would find him in the early hours of the morning. But, it wasn't nearly enough. He woke the next day with tears dried in his bloodshot eyes, struggling with the dark thoughts and emotions still lingering from the previous night.

The desire to run can become overwhelming. The desire to quit and find somewhere safe to hide can consume us. Through the tears, heartache and the battle for courage, God is present. He does not leave us in battle. In His presence is calm; and by His mercies we are not consumed. There is victory on the tomorrow side of the trial even if we can't see it today. Many times, God will bring people beside us to hold up our arms in battle just as Aaron and Hur did for Moses. *Exodus 17:11&12: "As long as Moses held up his hands, the Israelites were winning, but whenever he lowered his hands, the Amalekites were winning. When Moses' hands grew tired, they took a stone and put it under him and he sat on it. Aaron and Hur held his hands up—one on one side, one on the other—so that his hands remained steady till sunset."* (NIV1984) What joy and comfort! We may never fully know this side of Heaven; how God's saints will intervene on our behalf. Some are in the front lines of battle with us and others are holding up our hands through their prayers. Ultimately, it is, as told in *Deuteronomy 33:27: "The eternal God is thy refuge, and underneath are the everlasting arms."* (NIV1984) God is indeed our ultimate refuge. His arms do not tire from carrying the burdens of His children. Whatever burdens we may bear in this life, we can be assured that God bears them with us. If not, the weight of them would certainly consume our very soul.

Clarence thought of his dear friend, Pastor Wilson, as he drove to work on one of those days. On several occasions, he offered Clarence a gift of money. "There are so many great things during this time that God is doing to carry us through." Pastor Wilson would open his billfold and in earnest, speak to him. "Now, Clarence, I wish I had enough that I could bail you out completely." He often made the trip to the hospital to sit and pray with Clarence in some of his darkest moments, holding up Clarence's arms when he did not have strength, just as Aaron and Hur did for Moses. Patiently, faithfully, and without a hint of doubt, he assured Clarence and Beverly that God was able to see them through this trial. "Clarence, I believe God can bail you out in one day!" In his heart, Clarence had no doubt that God *could* bail them out in one day. Yet, he wondered when that time would come.

In truth, we've all experienced times of seeking evidence beyond what we could see and searching for blessings which were difficult to uncover within our circumstance. No doubt we have believed that God *is* capable of all things. The struggle to continue walking in faith begins when we wonder *if* He *will*. The precious father seeking healing for his son cried out to Jesus in *Mark 9:24*, exclaiming, *"Lord, I do believe; help me overcome my unbelief!" (NIV1984).* Clarence renewed his mind with these thoughts and restored his faith. Borrowing from his friend's bold proclamation and knowing that God's ways are just and perfect, as is written in *Deuteronomy 32:3-4*, he declared loudly as he drove, *"I will proclaim the name of the* LORD. *Oh, praise the greatness of our God! He is the Rock, His works are perfect, and all His ways are just. (NIV1984)*

15

COMING HOME

"Yet there is one ray of hope:
his compassion never ends."

— LAMENTATIONS 3:21-22 TLB

The pain woke Beverly in the middle of the night. She crawled out of bed, unable to stand. Something was very wrong. She had been battling, without telling anyone, spells of dizziness along with fatigue. But, this pain was something new. She made it to the phone. "Mom, I need you to come over to watch the kids." "Call the ambulance immediately, Beverly." "I'm on my way." She paged Clarence at Children's Hospital. "Beverly is being rushed to the hospital." Clarence left Mandy with the hospital staff in Columbus and rushed to meet Beverly at a nearby hospital. By the time she arrived, Beverly was doubled over, barely able to talk. The E.R. staff took her through the emergency room doors with Clarence running close behind. The doctors quickly examined her. "Burst fallopian tube. Internal bleeding." Clarence heard the doctors from the hallway. "Emergency surgery. Immediately. Hysterectomy."

Melody was the first to wake for school the next morning. "Grandma's sleeping on the couch." "Someone must be at the hospital." "Where's Mom?" "She's in the hospital, Melody. Go get your brothers and Molly. You'll stay with me after school for a while. The boys will stay with your Aunt." "Can we go see her?" "We'll see what the day brings. Go get ready for school now." Melody didn't want to go to school. She wanted to be with her mom. She went to see Molly in her crib. "It's going to be ok, Molly."

In the quiet of dawn, mercies are renewed. Darkness and dust from the previous day can be washed away, replaced with a spirit of victory and hope.

Clarence made the final turn into their driveway. He reached over to gently pat Beverly's hand while an involuntary sigh of relief escaped him. He looked over at his Bevie, eyes closed, resting. "She looks peaceful," but he knew the truth. "Exhausted." He closed his eyes in prayer. "Thank you, Lord, for this moment. For bringing us home. Thank you for my Bevie. Restore her health." Clarence held back his tears. "Good to go." That's what the doctor proclaimed over Beverly when he released her. Clarence knew she didn't feel "good to go". The physical and emotional toll that Mandy's illness had taken, coupled with the birth of Molly, the fear that had followed her birth, the physical pain and finally the removal of her womb, was physically too much to bear. But, Beverly Green was a woman of great faith in God's ability to make "all things good for those who serve and honor him." It was this unshakeable faith that enabled Beverly to renew her mind, body and spirit.

Beverly opened her eyes, which swelled with tears of gratitude, at the sight of their little home. The emotion of it caught her by surprise as she sat in the car for a moment taking everything in.

She could see her mother through the window standing at the kitchen sink, most likely washing dishes. It was just about time for Molly's afternoon nap and she imagined her sleeping peacefully in the playpen near the kitchen. Soon it would be time for the older children to return home from school. "Let's go inside," Clarence said as he helped her down from his truck. Beverly grew excited despite her weariness. It felt like ages since they had all been together as a family. "Tired, but joyful," she answered Clarence's unasked question, smiling as they walked into their home together. Clarence didn't feel like "shoutin' from the mountaintop," but having Beverly home was enough that he could strap on his boots and start another day. At this moment, all was well and he found himself humming:

Earthly friends may prove untrue,
Doubts and fears assail
One still loves and cares for you
One who will not fail

Though the sky be dark and drear
Fierce and strong the gale
Just remember He is near
And He will not fail

In life's dark and bitter hour
Love will still prevail
Trust His everlasting power
Jesus will not fail

Jesus never fails. Jesus never fails.
Heaven and earth may pass away.
But Jesus never fails.

Jesus Never Fails

— ARTHUR A. LUTHER - 1927

16

FAITH AND THE FIRE WALK

"...and he looked,
and behold, the bush burned with fire,
and the bush was not consumed."

— EXODUS 3:2 KJV

"There is no other choice?" Beverly looked skeptical. "What's it called?" "A Broviac line," the doctor answered. "It's a pretty routine process." "Nothing is ever routine with Mandy," Beverly replied. "It's necessary." "Her veins are worn down; flat. We cannot administer the medications any longer through them." "Essentially, we will create a tunnel to allow a tube to be inserted near her heart. It will carry blood and medicines to Mandy, just as an IV did through her arm." "It's a hard realization, Beverly. Without it, Mandy won't survive." Once again, they had no choice.

Clarence winced, later recalling Mandy's small body rejecting the Broviac catheter insertion four or five times, and developing an infection that created a hole in her skin the size of a nickel and ½″ deep. Slowly, Mandy healed from her infection and was able to come home. Clarence's mind took an inventory of events. He vividly recalled a particularly beautiful day in the Spring of 1983. He silently counted on his fingers, calculating that it would have been six months after Mandy's diagnosis that she could come home for a time. "She must have been about 19 months old when they pierced her heart with that thing." He felt himself getting tense and glanced again at Mandy to be sure she was still sleeping soundly. "It feels as if it happened yesterday." He remembered that day vividly.

Woody and Melody's game had ended abruptly as they heard their mom call from the kitchen, "Woody, pray!"and "Melody, grab the diapers!" Melody ran to get the cloth diapers and bucket as Woody dropped to his knees in prayer. Beverly quickly called her mother, the hospital and Pastor Wilson, and ran out the door carrying Mandy with Woody and Melody running close behind. In a matter of minutes, they were on their way to the hospital. "I need your help Melody," Beverly said, driving the only vehicle available that day, a manual, standard stick shift truck. Mandy was already bleeding badly from her nose and ears and struggling to breathe as she vomited oversized clots of blood. "It's far too much blood loss for such a small child." she thought. Mandy bled relentlessly while Melody, who had just turned 6 years old, sat next to her, mopping up Mandy's blood and exchanging bloody towels with Woody for clean ones. Beverly drove toward the hospital with only one thought, "Dear God, keep Mandy alive." "Keep praying Woody." "I am, Mommy." Woody said. "We're not going to make it in time," Beverly thought. She saw a police officer driving ahead of her. "If I can just get him to notice me, he might give me an escort to the hospital." She flashed her headlights, honked her horn and waved, but somehow, he seemed not to notice as she drove right past him.

She looked over at Mandy in the car seat, choking on her own blood. "Pray for green lights!" Finally, the 52 minute race ended and Beverly parked in front of the emergency doors. Leaving the truck, she swooped Mandy's lifeless body out of the car seat and ran inside. Melody couldn't move. She stood outside of the truck, staring at Mandy's car seat, dripping with her sister's blood; it looked like a crime scene with pools of Mandy's blood everywhere. This was their life. A mother, holding her daughter whose existence was slipping away with each drop of blood. Melody, her young daughter, forced herself to look away from the scene, but the memory was etched into her 6 year old mind. "Wait up, Woody!" Inside, Mandy's doctor shook his head, seemingly unable to find the right words. "Beverly, you should probably call Clarence. She isn't going to make it." "Yes she is!" Beverly said, staring the doctor down. "We need to get the platelets started. The nurse is trying to use the wrong needle. We need to get a butterfly 21 needle, that's the only one that works for Mandy."

Mandy had been at death's door many times since she was diagnosed. The doctors, based on her clinical condition, were obligated to tell her family that Mandy "isn't going to make it" and to "call her father and siblings to hurry to say their goodbyes." Beverly refused to give up or give in to the wishes of Mandy's doctors.

In the midst of heartache and our daily struggles, God's grace goes before us, paving the way for belief and courage. *Deuteronomy 31:8 "The LORD himself goes before you and will be with you; He will never leave you nor forsake you. Do not be afraid; do not be discouraged." (NIV1984)* His Word is clear. God knows we will have moments of fear and discouragement. He will go before us. Whatever path we are on, God has walked before us. We cannot imagine what the unseen side might look like if God did not pave the way for us to walk through the fire, one step at a time. We may stumble on rocks and trip over branches which have fallen, but He has gone before us to fill in the sinkholes and build bridges over crevices deep and dark. His grace has blazed the path for faith and belief to follow. Within the fire, God stands unwaveringly. The intensity of His love cleanses us. His love remains constant through the ages.

"Fasten me upon your heart as a seal of fire forevermore. This living, consuming flame will seal you as my prisoner of love. My passion is stronger than the chains of death and the grave, all consuming as the very flashes of fire from the burning heart of God. Place this fierce, unrelenting fire over your entire being. (Song of Songs 8:6 TPT).

NEAR DEATH'S DOOR

"But that's not all!
Even in times of trouble we have a joyful confidence,
knowing that our pressures will develop in us patient endurance.
And patient endurance will refine our character,
and proven character leads us back to hope."

— ROMANS 5:3-4 TPT

"I don't know how else to say it other than it's almost as if Mandy is out of life." Beverly told Clarence. "Life has just been drained out of her little body." Mandy had lost the ability to crawl. She was tottering around the furniture when she first got sick, but her body had been so weakened by treatments for this deadly illness that she had forgotten the things she previously learned. Mandy hadn't smiled much since the time of her diagnosis. She had been through so many traumas in her young life that she had never spoken; she was withdrawing from her short life of pain. As baby Molly grew older and was beginning to crawl, Mandy would look up at her mother as if to say, "What's she doing?" Beverly understood Mandy's language. "She can talk with her eyes and her fingers," she explained and went on to exclaim with the excited assurance of a mother's love. "Anybody can understand her!" Mandy would nod her head in agreement when she wanted to get down and try crawling. Soon, the two girls were playing together on a little picnic table and kitchenette that Beverly's sister bought them. This seemed normal to Beverly. They were over 2 ½ years into this daily battle and they were still standing. Mandy was still alive. And when Molly began to talk to Mandy, Mandy started talking to Molly.

On many nights, Clarence slept, but not soundly. Even in his dreams, his mind would not rest. He thought he heard Mandy cough. "Waiting for Mandy to bleed," he mentally noted. It was on everyone's mind, even if it wasn't always spoken. They all knew it was just a matter of time before another urgent trip to the hospital would be forthcoming, and the daily uncertainty wore on them. On this night, just as many others, as the family had long since fallen asleep, Clarence heard Mandy cough again. This time he was sure he was not dreaming. He forced his eyes open. "4:00 a.m." Mandy wasn't coughing, she was choking! Clarence jumped out of the bed, quickly picked up his Mandy and headed for the door. He shouted toward Beverly that he was heading to the hospital. Beverly, who had been deep asleep, was wide awake in an instant. "I will stay with Molly," she said. "Take Walter with you!" Walter's instincts, hard wired after so many trips to the hospital, kicked in immediately. He was wide awake in moments. Walter dressed, grabbed the bucket, towels and diapers, and jumped into the truck. Clarence was in the driver seat ready to go. Walter climbed over next to Mandy. He immediately grabbed one of the cloth diapers to try and stop the blood that was now flowing rapidly from Mandy's nose, mouth and ears. The same question popped into his young mind, as it

NEAR DEATH'S DOOR | 71

did at the beginning of every trip to the hospital. "What if we don't make it in time?"

They drove on the highway into the dark of night. There was an air of intense silence as both Walter and Clarence were too frightened and exhausted to talk to one another. Clarence glanced over to briefly check on Mandy and Walter. Walter locked eyes with his father. "We'll make it Walter," Clarence said as he checked his rearview mirror. "Wait, did I miss the exit?" He and Walter both realized what had happened at the same moment. The barrier wall loomed beside them on their left, sealing their fate. They were trapped. There was no way off the highway for another 10 minutes. This would add another 20 minutes to their trip. Clarence pressed the pedal. "Please God, don't let this be the time we don't make it. Please, not on my watch." Walter prayed silently to himself as he continued what felt like a losing battle, sopping up Mandy's blood which flowed into the truck's seat and onto the floor.

"How did I do this? What was I thinking? One slip up and I'm on a road I never intended to take. I've driven these roads dozens of times." His thoughts intensified to the point of panic. "Please God, not this time." He prayed silently, unknowingly mirroring Walter's prayer as he exited, looped around the next off ramp and re-entered the highway. Walter silently counted the minutes lost from missing the exit while calculating the remaining distance to the hospital as he cared for Mandy who was now violently coughing up blood clots. Clarence vacillated between prayer and beating himself up for missing the exit. Finally, they saw the sign. Columbus Children's Hospital - 1 mile. They were almost there. Walter held his breath as Clarence pulled off the exit and onto the adjacent road that would take them to the emergency room entrance. Walter looked down at Mandy. His sister was limp, pale, exhausted and seemingly lifeless. "She's really bad, Dad." All Walter could think about is how close they were to losing Mandy. He felt numb

They entered the E.R. entrance. It was 5:15 a.m. when this miracle train, despite missing a turn, was right on time. Walter knew his mom would be arriving at the hospital soon. The moment she did, he and his father would leave the hospital and go directly to work. For now, there was nothing to do but wait as the blood slowly dripped into Mandy's IV. He felt his eyes getting heavy as he settled deeper into the chair and dozed off.

As Walter and Clarence waited at the hospital, Woody was waking up at home. Walter's younger brother was unaware of the early morning events which had taken place. He laid in bed for a few moments until he remembered what day it was. "Family day!" Woody looked over and saw brother Wayne sleeping, but Walter was gone. "He must be up already," Woody surmised as he ran out of his bedroom. This was the day he was waiting for; a planned day filled with fun with his family. Activities and games had been in the making for the car ride, snacks along the way and food for a picnic lunch, all in pursuit of adventure and discovery at the world renowned Columbus Zoo. More than anyone, Woody loved to have fun with his family. But the house seemed strangely quiet to him. He had expected to see his mother in the kitchen getting breakfast ready before the family hit the road. "I must be the first one up," He turned the corner into the family room and stopped suddenly as he saw his Grandmother lying on the couch. He was crushed and couldn't stop the tears that welled up in his eyes. He knew what this meant. The promise of the day was cancelled.

"These are the moments that build character, Woody," Clarence would say. "Times like these will shape your life and the lives of our family. How we view and respond to the mountains and valleys of life is the best test of character." "These times will mold you into the man you will become." Clarence paused for a moment. "Have faith, son."

A LAZARUS MOMENT

"When the Lord saw her,
his heart went out to her and he said,
"Don't cry."

— LUKE 7:13 NIV1984

"Knock on wood!" the doctor said. "Mandy is stable." Beverly smiled. "It's not wood, it's God." "Another day of life. Another day of God's promises fulfilled." Beverly was never shy about her faith. She was grateful this day, and, as always, somewhat astonished that Mandy was able to rest while hooked up to tubes and IVs. "Her little body must be entirely spent." Beverly could see traces of blood in Mandy's hair, but apart from the IV, there was not much visible evidence of the battle from the night before. Her color was returning. "Don't be anxious, Beverly." she heard God say. "I'm just exhausted, Lord." The treatments that were supposed to be helping Mandy appeared to be taking the life out of her, little by little. Endless medicines, chemotherapy and other experimental drugs were powerful therapies for little Mandy to endure. "I know the doctors are doing their best. This is a rare and horrible disease with no cure. I think they are simply making their best judgement, but every decision is a matter of life or death now." She waited, with all the patience she could muster, for a reply from God.

"Well, there is a lot that is praiseworthy," she thought. Beverly wondered if there were some in her extended family that were having their faith tested. She intuitively knew some people were asking the obvious question, addressing the so-called elephant in the room. "Well, where is your God?" She was surprised at this thought. "I guess I can understand that, based on the visible." God's presence was so evident to Beverly, even in her darkest and most fearful moments. It never occurred to her that He had forsaken Mandy or her family. She had heard His voice since she was a child. She heard the angels singing for her. She was steadfast in her understanding and wholly aware of the mission that was given to their family: "Keep Mandy alive, at all costs." The worldly price for this mission was high- emotionally, physically and financially. There were now five other children to care for. Yet, each time Mandy survived another battle, it was more evidence of God's presence and plan. She listened to the voice inside her. "I know your heart breaks for Mandy. I know you feel her pain, as well as her joy." Beverly felt God's peace, in the deepest place of her soul, mingled with the ache and sorrow of the day. But there was no other place she would rather be than in the hands of her loving God. "It's just that, we can't see the end of the story - the other side of the mountain." Finally, Beverly heard God's reply. "Lay it down. I am in control. Didn't I tell you I would see you through?"

By the time Beverly returned home late that evening, the house was quiet and still. All Beverly wanted to do was wash away the day in a warm bath and put Mandy to bed for badly needed rest.

A LAZARUS MOMENT | 75

She looked at Mandy, and was shaken. This illness, at times, caused the skin between Mandy's fingers and toes to "melt away" due to ongoing blood loss. There were days when Mandy's teeth would become loose. Mandy would often suffer from "petechiae," which caused little red spots to appear all over her body due to the hemorrhaging of the capillaries. In one terrifying incident, Mandy's little ear had almost fallen off, where the histiocytes had chewed through her skin. Blood was God's tool for keeping the human body intact, and Mandy's body could not retain the exact measure of it to keep her going.

"Where is God?" In times of need, we acknowledge and understand that God responds to us in His word. We are assured of His constant presence. He does not forget His children during times of trouble. In this life, we will have tribulation. But, God has promised to walk with us through it. His heart breaks with ours in pain and in loss. He feels our hurt as well as our joy. He is ever present in the lives of His children. *Luke 12:6 proclaims, "Are not five sparrows sold for two pennies? Yet not one is forgotten before God. Indeed, the very hairs of your head are all numbered. Don't be afraid; you are worth more than many sparrows."* (NIV1984) The abiding comfort of His presence, combined with the assurance that there is no better place to be than in the hands of a loving God, is our path to peace while on this earth.

As Beverly finally began to fall asleep, she whispered to him, "How long?", Lord. Her answer came in the recollection of *Psalm 13:1-2.* *"O LORD, how long will you forget me? Forever? How long will you look the other way? How long must I struggle with anguish in my soul, with sorrow in my heart every day?"* (NLT) Yet, still, she would not allow frustration, fear or anger to momentarily blind her from seeing God's grace. For this day, His grace had been sufficient. Beverly weathered her trials knowing that God is who He says He is, and that He would do what He said He would do. He promised her long ago that He would see her family through these days. She was unwavering in this belief, and it gave her the enduring strength of an entire army of angels. Her faith never wavered. If God had made a more faithful person than Beverly Green, he was keeping her identity a secret.

19

THE KILLING CURE

"After he said to Thomas,
Put thy finger here, and see mine hands,
and put forth thine hand, and put it into my side,
and be not faithless, but faithful."

— JOHN 20:27 GNV)

"We've always dreamed of a family vacation to Disney," Beverly said to the nurse. "We are coordinating with 'Make a Wish' on your behalf. They are offering your family a dream trip." She knew the reason the trip was being offered. Doctors had determined, once again, that ultimately, Mandy would not survive. "I see all the evidence," she said to Clarence later. "But I refuse to give power to any voice other than God's." "It's His promise that has carried us through this far." Clarence agreed. "It's His word which has sustained Mandy's every breath and given us strength to lift our arms in praise." Moments when it appeared all was lost, they continued to bring their prayers before God with full expectation that He would answer.

By spring of 1984, Mandy's condition had deteriorated once again. The histiocytes continued to ravage her body. Mandy's lymph glands were severely swollen and the need for blood transfusions became a nearly daily event. "You have to be prepared for the worst," Mandy's doctor said. "We are prepared for what God has promised us," Beverly replied. She continued to talk hopefully with the nurses about a family trip to Disney as soon as Mandy could travel.

"Are we really going to Disney, Dad?" Woody asked. "We are praying for that, Woody." Clarence said. "We know God likes a good celebration, too!" The Green household was filled with excitement as the children imagined a trip to Florida, the beach and the magic of Disney World. The doctors and nurses began coordinating with Make a Wish to put measures in place for Mandy's treatments and traveling. But airports, air travel, amusement parks; all of it created too many risks. What if something happened while Mandy was in flight? What if they were at the airport, a beach or inside Disney and Mandy began to bleed? There were simply too many "What if scenarios." Logistically, no matter how hard everyone tried, this trip was impossible. The children were accustomed to plans changing and the cancelling of fun, but this time, it was a crushing disappointment to them. Refusing to give up, the nurses and doctors continued to work with Make a Wish and a trip was finally arranged for the family to visit Port Clinton, Ohio. "It's not Disney," Beverly said when they arrived, "but it's just perfect." She loved the little lakefront cottage as soon as she saw it. When the children discovered the private deck leading to the beach behind the cottage, their cheers, hoots and hollers filled her and Clarence's hearts with joy. Medical care, in an abundance of caution, had been arranged for Mandy at a nearby hospital.

"Well, if this isn't heaven, I don't know what is." Clarence said. "Me and my boys, all together, on a private, chartered fishing boat." The boys proudly brought their fish back to their mother at the cottage. "Goodness, look at that!" They celebrated each day in that little cottage on the beach, grilling and eating outside on the patio, packing picnics and driving golf carts to explore the island. The backyard too, was fully equipped with swing sets, a basketball court and any activity a young child could imagine.

Molly cheerfully went about the business of quietly entertaining her parents, siblings and anyone who happened to be in the room. It was wonderful and for a few days, the thought of losing Mandy was not the topic of conversation. In spite of the looming news from the doctors, which had not changed, they returned home rejuvenated - and hopeful. Yet, it didn't take long for life to resume the new 'normal' when they returned from the trip. The older children prepared for their final days of school. Clarence resumed his long work hours as each day seemed to roll into the next. Mandy's condition remained fragile and trips to the hospital did not cease.

Beverly heard God speaking to her heart in May of 1984 when she was giving Mandy her penicillin. "Don't do that." The words came again. As she heard His voice speaking to her heart, she became afraid. "This doesn't make sense." she thought. But Beverly knew she had heard God's voice clearly. She mustered the courage and faith to sit in stillness to hear His voice. She understood God's direction. *"Whenever I am afraid, I will trust in You."* The words of the Psalmist in 56:3 came to her. She wasn't going to quit trusting God. Beverly trusted God's voice above the fear, and stopped giving the prescribed penicillin to Mandy. Two months later, Beverly sat with Mandy's doctor, praying he wouldn't ask her about the administration of this drug. No such luck. "Are you still giving Mandy the penicillin?" Beverly truthfully answered, "No." "What?"

The good Doctor couldn't help himself. He was, at first, angry and disappointed. He was personally invested in the Green family's fight for their daughter. He had seen them countless times over these past years. His heart broke along with theirs with every battle that Mandy fought, rejoiced over every battle won and he longed for that one day when, he would be able to give the family the good news they had hoped for. But now, he was gravely concerned. "Nurse, please bring me Mandy's chart." He reviewed it for a while as Beverly sat and watched. "Lord, please, let this be good news." The doctor looked up from the chart and shook his head. "I'm baffled." "Mandy's numbers are improving." "As a doctor, I'm telling you to give it to her." Then, putting his hand on Beverly's shoulder, under his breath he said, "As a friend, you did the right thing."

Oftentimes, we earnestly seek to understand circumstances or events before they have completely unfolded. We battle impatiently and fear clings to us until we see for ourselves, the final outcome - and purpose. But, God does not say we will never have fear. He says, He will never leave us or forsake us. God's fingerprints are all over our lives - we only need vigilance to see them. As often as we pray, God is faithful to answer. He directs our attention to Himself as the source of the proof. There will be no moment in our lives, authored by God, which will be mistaken for an accident. He doesn't leave small, concealed clues - the prints He leaves behind are found in His love, grace and hope that are present in every circumstance in our lives. *"But now, O Lord, thou art our Father: we are the clay, and thou art our potter, and we all are the work of thine hands."* *(Isaiah 64:8 GNV)* Just as the lives of those around us reveal evidence of our own love and actions, our Heavenly Father's divine authorship is imprinted and evident in the lives of His children.

20

BREATHLESS

"But Jesus beheld them, and said unto them,
with men this is impossible;
but with God all things are possible."

— MATTHEW 19:26, KJV

C larence and Beverly huddled together under the cozy blanket. They were both exhausted. Yet, alone together in their favorite spot by the bonfire, they quietly celebrated the day. Breathing in the cool night air and enjoying the view of the stars, Clarence exclaimed to his bride, "What a moment!" Beverly smiled, nodding in agreement, "Mandy sure does love shocking us." she said. Clarence chuckled at that. "All things possible, and the countless moments in between which seem impossible," God is the Author of them all. Beverly and Clarence had agonized in prayer over their decision to stop all experimental treatments, medications and chemotherapy. The treatments were draining the life out of their little girl, which seemed to Beverly and Clarence equal to the horrible effects of the disease itself. Today, God had given them hope along with blessed encouragement that their decision was the correct one. Clarence looked toward their little house as he often did when sitting in this spot. He smiled at the little pink tricycle parked beneath a tree. "Yes, this has been a good day,"he said.

Mandy was 3 years old now and could not walk on her own. It was suggested to Beverly that it would be more convenient and suitable for Mandy to have a wheelchair. "Most likely, she will never walk again," the doctor said. "I will never agree to a wheelchair! I believe my daughter will walk." Beverly would hold Mandy's hands, encourage her to take a few steps and applaud every effort her daughter made. Every tiny step, along with the look of determination on Mandy's face told a greater story and revealed the spirit of determination which God had placed within her. Mandy was a fighter, just like her mom. Together, they prayed, along with their church congregation. United in purpose, they proclaimed God's faithfulness and gave thanks for His loving help. "Help Mandy in a mighty way so that all those who are watching will witness Your power and glory." Beverly prayed.

That morning, Beverly sat in the familiar little room near the emergency entrance with Mandy resting in her arms, waiting for the nurse. Mandy was peaceful for the moment and Beverly breathed a sigh of relief. She gently laid Mandy on the little bed, knowing she would not have the strength to get down on her own. She stepped out for a quick peek into the hall outside to check on the other children. "They must be starving." She had no money to buy food. The lunch she had prepared was left at home in their rush to leave and would have to substitute for their dinner. She found Woody and Melody playing quietly in a waiting room just down the hall with baby Molly. She looked out the window and saw the hot dog truck that sometimes came to the hospital to sell lunches. Occasionally, Beverly would have a spare dollar or two and would treat the children to a hot dog, but today she simply assured them that dinner would be waiting for them when they got home. Melody did her best to hide her disappointment and tears as her belly grumbled. She looked over at Woody for encouragement. Woody smiled and whispered, "It's going to be ok." He had found a ketchup packet under the seat in the car which he shared with Melody on the ride to the hospital. "Maybe I'll find a few more for the ride home."

Beverly turned the corner into the little room where she had left Mandy. The room was empty. "I was only gone for a moment, how did I miss the nurse?" They must have started her platelets already, she thought. "But why would they take Mandy without letting me know? Didn't the nurse see me down the hall? I was only gone for a few moments." Beverly continued, not realizing she was speaking her thoughts out loud. She turned to leave the room and almost ran into the nurse. "Where is Mandy?" Beverly asked, confused. The nurse looked just as baffled as Beverly. "I don't know, I thought she was here with you." Beverly tried not to panic. Where could she have gone? And then, as mysterious as her disappearance, rounding the corner, riding a three wheeler for the first time in her life, was little Mandy Green! They all stared, speechless. The sight of Mandy riding that little bike, and even more miraculously, using her little feet on the floor to pedal that tricycle, was a miracle. Mandy moved happily toward them as they all cheered her on as she stopped directly in front of her mother. Beverly reached down to pick up her daughter. God had heard her prayer. God helped Mandy in a mighty way for all to witness. Excitement filled the hospital that day as the story was told to nurses and doctors. Later, Mandy's doctor came to see Beverly. "Tell Clarence to get Mandy a tricycle to ride every day. Doctor's prescription!" Clarence went immediately after work and bought

Mandy her very own pink tricycle with sparkled tassels and parked it under the tree along with the other childrens' bikes. Beverly and Clarence praised God as they sat together, smiling at the little bike and all that it represented; Hope, victory and the assurance of God's presence in the battle.

WE'RE FRESH OUT

"You've kept track of all my wandering and my weeping.
You've stored my many tears in your bottle—not one will be lost.
For they are all recorded in your book of remembrance."

— PSALM 56:8 TPT

L ittle by little, day by day, almost imperceptibly, Mandy was gaining strength. She was learning to play and would laugh so loudly during "hide and seek" that the other children always knew when she had found someone. It was as though she was discovering her world for the very first time. Her exuberant personality, kept hidden during years of trauma and treatments, was now flourishing and on full display. Her legs were getting stronger from riding her tricycle. Soon, she was able to stand. Doctors fitted her with leg braces from her feet to her knees. Daily exercise, combined with the support of her leg braces, worked. By March of 1986, Mandy was learning to walk.

"Mandy is walking now." Beverly informed God aloud, as if He wasn't aware. She was making the familiar drive to get Mandy's platelet levels checked. "What a parade of miracles!" she said, glancing at Mandy as she pulled onto the highway. "I really wouldn't trade any of it." Beverly mused, as she continued her personal conversation with God. "We're living our dream. A simple home filled with love and family." "It looks different than what I imagined." "But, thank you, God, for entrusting Mandy to us." "Almost there, Mandy." she said.

The doctors finally found a way to keep Mandy alive - simply maintain her platelets at a level high enough so that she didn't bleed out. On this day, Beverly did not expect that it would be any different from the trips she had made in the recent past. Draw Mandy's blood. Check her platelet levels. Wait, while she received the life sustaining blood. "Good morning, Mandy." The nurse greeted them as they made their way down the familiar corridor and into the nondescript hospital room. "Something's wrong." Beverly said silently as the nurse prepared to draw Mandy's blood. Nothing in the routine had changed. "Something feels off." The nurse avoided eye contact with her. "The doctor will be back soon with the results." the nurse said as she left the room. Beverly closed her eyes and held Mandy close. She gently stroked her hair, rocked back and forth and began to pray.

The doctor cleared his throat, interrupting Beverly's silent prayers. Looking into his eyes, she saw his tears. Her heart sank. He looked down at the floor for a few moments before looking back at Beverly. "The hospital will not be able to supply Mandy's blood products for much longer." "We have sustained the process for 4 years and the time is coming soon when we will not be able to continue; the insurance company will not cover Mandy's expenses beyond the first year of treatments and the hospital cannot

continue to support the cost of her treatments. I'm sorry, Beverly."
"Impossible!" Beverly said.

The very treatment that was keeping Mandy alive would no longer be available. Beverly's heart was broken. She had seen her daughter hemorrhage enough times to know what the end of this story would now be. She also knew that it wouldn't be long before the platelets that Mandy had within her would die. "When?" she asked. He shook his head. "It's not certain." Beverly sat, waiting for Mandy to receive her blood. She drove home from the hospital later in silence and prayer, clinging to the only hope that they had ever had for Mandy. God had promised to see them through. He had carried them through their trials again and again. Heartbroken, the words came softly. *"Be merciful to me, O LORD, for I am in distress; my eyes grow weak with sorrow, my soul and my body with grief. My life is consumed by anguish.* "(Psalm 31:9-10a, NIV1984)

She couldn't bring herself to get out of the car. She saw Clarence through the kitchen window. He smiled and waved for her to come in. Earlier, she had prepared the only food that was left in their home. Hamburger casserole, prepared with the last of their meat and milk. Beverly took a deep breath, lifted Mandy out of the car and began the short walk to the door. "This will not be Mandy's story," she proclaimed. "Dinner's warm." She didn't have the heart to tell any of them the news she had just heard. Another deep breath. "I'll carry it," Walter said, grabbing the bowl of hamburger helper. "I've got the napkins," Melody chimed in, just in time to watch the bowl slip out of Walter's hands and onto the floor. Glass and hamburger meat crashed to the floor. Meat and shards of glass were everywhere. "What now?" Melody asked. They all knew that was the last of the food in the pantry, and most likely, there was no money left to buy more. In the middle of the chaos, Woody quietly began looking under couch cushions, then expanding his search to every corner of the house, mining for spare change. Miraculously, hidden in cushions, pockets, drawers and underneath beds, was just enough money to order a pizza that night for dinner.

"I need to talk with you, Clarence." Beverly's voice trembled as she recounted the day's events. Clarence listened to Beverly's rocking news. "So, everything we've been fighting against, the debts, hospital bills, insurance, living paycheck to paycheck. It's all for nothing now?" Anger overwhelmed him and he began asking questions to which Beverly had no answers. We've given every dollar we have to keep our daughter alive; and now, we are being told that it isn't enough! This is unbelievable!" He felt as though he had been punched in the gut. Clarence continued his outburst. "The hospital has just issued Mandy's death sentence." Tears burned his eyes and he could find no words of encouragement as he looked at his bride. "We've got nothing left," he said. Bevie offered, "We still have our Mandy." Clarence stared off into the corner. All was quiet. Each day must end. Soon, the family retired for the night.

22

IN THE FOG OF WAR

"When the servant of the man of God got up early the next morning
and went outside,
there were troops, horses, and chariots everywhere.
"Oh, sir, what will we do now?"
the young man cried to Elisha.

— 2 KINGS 6:15 NLT

E lisha's young servant, Elijah, awoke early in the morning
and found that his soldiers were encompassed by the
enemy. Many times in this life we find ourselves in the
same difficulties as Elisha's men. There are times when the enemy,
like a thief in the night, enters our household and seeks to do harm
to ourselves or our family. We are blindsided by this unanticipated
challenge, unprepared, confused and without defense as we come
face to face with such threatening harm. In times like these we feel
alone, outnumbered and are overwhelmed in thought by the
insurmountable forces stacked against us. No matter how hard we
try, we cannot see through the fog of battle. In times like these, we

ask ourselves, "Have I been abandoned? " "Are you there, God?" "Do you see me?" "Have you heard my prayers?"

Seasons in life may come that will leave us weary. There will be no tears left to cry and we fear our prayers have gone unanswered. We ask, "Why would a loving God allow His children to suffer?" Doubt creeps in. In the fog of war, doubt springs eternal. "Are the promises of God after all, just words in a book?" Our redemption comes through faith in Him. It is His Heavenly vision which cuts through the fog. Elisha prayed for Elijah *"Don't be afraid!" Elisha told him. "For there are more on our side than on theirs!Then Elisha prayed, "O God, open his eyes and let him see." The eyes of the young man were opened and he saw. A wonder! The whole mountainside full of horses and chariots of fire surrounding Elisha!"* (2 Kings 6:16-17 MSG) God's army.

When God gives a promise, it does not necessarily follow that we will receive it immediately. We have to claim the promise, stepping out in faith, even in doubt, when we cannot see the outcome of our battle. This is the overriding theme in the story of the Israelites journey into the promised land. This journey of faith challenged His people for a long period of time as they wandered through the wilderness. The people complained against Moses and Aaron. *"Why didn't God let us die in comfort in Egypt where we had lamb stew and all the bread we could eat?"* (Exodus 16:3 MSG)

There came a time when God's people crossed over the Jordan where God set them on firm ground once again. *Joshua 3:17 "Then the priests who bore the ark of the covenant of the Lord stood firm on dry ground in the midst of the Jordan; and all Israel crossed over on dry ground, until all the people had crossed completely over the Jordan."* (NKJV) Yet, after the crossing, a battle to secure the promise was still ahead; the walls of Jericho had to come down. Like the Israelites, there are times when we can't see a way through. There is no turning back. Faith demands that we move forward with belief in God's covenant when our hearts are broken and our faith is fleeting. The Green family walked through the fire, trusting God, one day at a time, one step at a time, one moment at a time. They put on the full armor of God and marched to the promised land.

We are called to a faith that is bold enough to ask and trust. In the asking, we are promised daily mercy and grace in our time of need. *Hebrews 4:16 "Let us therefore come boldly unto the throne of grace that we may obtain mercy, and find grace to help in time of need." (KJV)* The Greens prayed without ceasing for delivery from their circumstance. Prayer was their weapon of choice. It permitted them to see through the fog of war. Prayer lights the spark of hope. It drives our passions and is proof of our faith. Hope is, as paraphrased from the *Webster 1828 dictionary; "A desire for good… accompanied by a belief or expectation of obtaining it. Since hope implies the possibility of possessing the good desired, it always gives pleasure or joy. A wish or desire without hope may be accompanied by pain and anxiety. In contrast, hopelessness despairs and has no expectation of good."* Hope is the expectation of obtaining what is good. We have all been given this gift of prayer to choose as our weapon, as the Green family did, in times of crisis. God's Word stands as a testimony of His grace, and ultimately we can stand faithfully on our own in Christ and receive this truth as it is stated in *Romans 15:13: "I pray that God, the source of hope, will fill you completely with joy and peace because you trust in Him. Then you will overflow with confident hope through the power of the Holy Spirit." (NLT)*

One faithful evening, Beverly went to the Wednesday evening church service with her children to see Pastor Wilson and claim the promise God had given to her. "I will see you through." She sat quietly with Mandy, waiting until the end of the service. Turning to leave, Pastor Wilson saw Beverly sitting with Mandy behind the piano. His smile faded as Beverly shared everything the doctor told her. It was now time for bold prayer and proclamation. The other children watched with their mother as Pastor Wilson immediately knelt down beside Mandy and wrapped his arms around her tiny waist. They surrounded Mandy and prayed with Pastor Wilson as he boldly asked God to help her produce her own blood. After a long period of time, Beverly quietly gathered her children together for the return ride home. There was a silence during the ride home. Mandy and Molly were fast asleep leaving Beverly and the other children lost in their own thoughts. Beverly prayed, then broke the silence. "God is faithful and loving." "Lord, if you want us to keep Mandy, make it in such a fashion that only you can get glory for it." Amen.

23

THE COST OF LOVE

"And now these three remain:
faith, hope and love.
But the greatest of these is love."

— 1 CORINTHIANS 13:13 NIV1984

There are a multitude of passages in the Bible that speak to God's love. *1 John 4:19 "We love Him, because He first loved us." (KJV)* He loved me first. He knew me first. And the proof of His love is shown by His great sacrifice. *1 John 4:9-11 "This is how God showed His love among us: He sent His one and only Son into the world that we might live through Him. This is love; not that we loved God, but that He loved us and sent His Son as an atoning sacrifice for our sins. Dear friends, since God so loved us, we also ought to love one another." (NIV1984)* Love paid the price that I could not pay; love always comes at a price. But, what is the cost of love?

Clarence and Beverly found themselves driving to Columbus, by order of the IRS, once again. Lost in his own thoughts, Clarence glanced at the worn cardboard file box sitting between him and Beverly. The box was overflowing with papers, receipts and bills. He felt about as worn out as the box looked. The cost of Mandy's treatments financially broke them. "This shouldn't feel normal", he said aloud to Beverly who was lost in her own thoughts in the passenger seat. Somehow this familiar drive to Columbus for another IRS audit and hearing, just like the drives to the hospital for Mandy's treatments, had become another odd sort of normal in their lives. He reached over the box for Beverly's hand. She was quiet. "We have surely been through it", he thought. These two young kids, who long ago promised before God to give their lives to each other, had no idea where the journey of life would lead them. Here they were, together, facing financial disaster as a thought came to Clarence. "None of this matters."

A new question formed in his mind, "What is the cost of love?" He thought about this for a while as he continued to drive in silence. "There is always a price, always a sacrifice." Clarence continued to voice his thoughts. "If there is no cost to love, a sacrifice or some act, then where is the proof of love?", he went on to wonder. "Mandy is alive," he and Beverly whispered to one another in synchronicity. Nothing else mattered to them. The entire Green family had been willing to make the sacrifice, the gift for them was priceless; Mandy. From the youngest to the oldest, hours of prayer, days of uncertainty and endless weekends sitting with Mandy in the hospital, were proof of their commitment.

"It's a miracle," Clarence said. "She hasn't had another drop of blood." Day by day, the joyful realization came to the Green family that Mandy was healing. Each visit to the doctor confirmed that Mandy was producing her own blood. She was growing stronger. Mandy was soon able to walk, run and play with the help of her leg braces. She slowly recovered from the physical and psychological trauma of her battle. "It's just been a parade of miracles", Beverly proclaimed. It felt like they were on the brink of seeing the other side of the mountain.

The roller coaster, however, continued. Hours later, it was clear. *The Green's made the prayerful decision to always pay Mandy's hospital bills first. They relied on God's word to deliver them from the balance of their financial hardships.* But on this day, they could see no way out of their financial dilemma that came with Mandy's illness. The IRS auditor, after reviewing the claim for payment, matter of factly listed his findings. Bankruptcy was the only option. Clarence's masonry business would be gone. No forgiveness of any tax debt, would be in the offing this day. There would be more audits to come. The Greens would be required to show proof of every penny earned and spent. In the end, the reality set in that they would lose their family home; it would be auctioned off. The Greens left the meeting in silence, stunned. For 4 ½ years, they had not wavered in their mission. "Keep Mandy alive. No matter the cost, no matter the sacrifice." The mission was fulfilled; the cost had been great. Clarence drove from Columbus directly to Pastor Wilson's home. Pastor Wilson took a knee, tears streaming down his face, and openly prayed what he felt to be true. This good man, in a most personal conviction, knew the truth. "If God can heal Mandy, he can save your home," he declared.

Emotionally drained, Clarence and Beverly returned home. Their family home for the past eleven years was a place of laughter, prayers and togetherness. Bolstered by faith, they held onto the bold prayer which their Pastor had prayed. They knew they were on borrowed time unless God intervened. "Every day, God has been faithful in His provision," Clarence said. "Every need has been met." *"And when the layer of dew lifted, there, on the surface of the wilderness, was a small round substance, as fine as frost on the ground. So when the children of Israel saw it, they said to one another, "What is it?" For they did not know what it was. And Moses said to them, "This is the bread which the Lord has given you to eat." (Exodus 16:14-15 NKJV)*

We don't always recognize Heavenly bread. God's provision does not always come in a form that is familiar to us or one that we would desire. But God is clear in His Word. He *will* provide for His people. Faith requires a willingness to continue when we don't think we can. The continuing verses of *Exodus 16* give instruction for gathering manna. *v.16 "This is the thing which the Lord has commanded: 'Let every man gather it according to each one's need, one omer for each person, according to the number of persons; let every man take for those who are in his tent.'" (NKJV)* God provides for each person according to their need. Just as the Israelites did, the Greens worked to gather what God gave them each day, with nothing carrying over. *"So the people of Israel did as they were told. Some gathered a lot, some only a little. But when they measured it out, everyone had just enough. Those who gathered a lot had nothing left over, and those who gathered only a little had enough. Each family had just what it needed." (NLT)* Nothing carried over. (*v.17-18*) Finally, in *Exodus 16:19 & 20* Moses said, *"Let no one leave any of it till morning." Notwithstanding they did not heed Moses. But some of them left part of it until morning, and it bred worms and stank. (NKJV)*

Some of what we experience day to day, if allowed to carry over, will breed darkness in our lives. There are items that should be gathered daily and the effects compound for good when they carry over. "Faith, hope and love." Others, we would be better off leaving behind, purging them for good; pride and unbelief. We all have our own unique and personal struggles. God's Word is the source of daily bread for our souls. He provides manna for our daily physical needs and abundant grace for our daily spiritual needs. The well of His love never runs dry and the wellspring of hope carries a full portion of new mercies. And so, we praise Him. Clarence and Beverly walked hand in hand into their home. Lifting her other hand, Beverly praised God, *"Not to us, O LORD, not to us but to Your name be the glory, because of Your love and faithfulness." (Psalm 115:1 NIV1984)*

24

STIRRED, NOT SHAKEN

"I will proclaim the name of the LORD.
Oh, praise the greatness of our God!"

— DEUTERONOMY 32:3 NIV1984

Clarence stared into the little fire pit where for the past 12 years, he and Beverly had spent almost every spring and summer evening with their 6 children. "We burned through more wood during the summer months than winter," he thought. The smell of roasted hot dogs seemed to linger as memories of hide and seek, laughter, games and bonfires flooded his mind. They didn't have TV. "We're living life in 3D," he told the children. The sky and the stars provided the backdrop to their family's story time. Clarence always assumed that this would be their forever home. "Has time really passed so quickly?" He and Bevie just celebrated their 16 year wedding anniversary. It seemed like only a moment ago when he asked his bride to spend the rest of her life with him. He glanced away from the fire pit toward their little house and smiled. He could see Beverly and some of the children in the kitchen from where he was sitting.

That morning, Clarence watched as his Mandy was taking her first step toward a normal life and what she had been dreaming of. "What a victory!" Clarence shouted as Mandy waited for the school bus in the driveway with Beverly and Molly, one hand clutching her mother's hand and the other clutching her brand new lunchbox. She was beaming with excitement and anticipation. "Go get 'em Mandy," Clarence said, giving her a bear hug as he headed off to work. Beverly watched, through joyful tears, as her daughter found her seat and continued watching until the bus was out of sight. Mandy had taken her very first steps toward a journey away from the watchful eyes of her mother, family and doctors. But the final battle of this spiritual warfare was just getting started.

As the school bus drove out of sight, the county sheriff pulled into the Green's driveway. "So, this is the day", she thought to herself. "I'm sorry, ma'am." Reality settled into Beverly's heart as she watched him work his way through their home, quietly taking notes, appraising their belongings for the auction. "The auction is scheduled for Friday, October 16th," he said. "I'm really sorry," he mumbled again. She led him to the door. In a recent recurring dream, Beverly had received a message about, of all things, a television. "I'm going to use television to bail you out." God told her. What does that mean?" Beverly asked. "Lord, you know we don't own a TV. I don't want one and I don't want anything to do with it." She dialed Clarence's pager and waited for him to return her call. Despite being perplexed by her dream, she surrendered to God. "If television is the tool You choose to bail us out, I will submit to it."

"Wish you were here, friend." Clarence said into the fire pit. His first impulse had been to call Pastor Wilson, but he passed on earlier that year. "We could use your prayers, right about now." Clarence echoed his Pastor's bold declaration, "God, I believe you can bail the Green family out in one day!" Looking around, he realized that not much had changed since 1975. Their neighbors generously shared the pasture field to the left and the hay field in front of them, making their one acre feel much larger. "We've had a blessed life here," he said, laughing out loud as he remembered swinging with Beverly, getting carried away to the point of breaking the swing and sending them both onto the ground. Beverly's shouts of "Goodness, Clarence," echoed in the silence of this present moment. He smiled as he looked at the much stronger swing he'd built to accommodate them.

The Greens were humble people, faithful people and above all, God loving people. They took joy in life's simple pleasures. That was the beauty of it all. Their home wasn't luxurious, large or worth much on the real estate market, but it was rich in memories. They always taught their children that a "house" was not a "home." They were short on the house part, but over the top on what builds a "home;" Love, honoring God and commitment to one another. Yet, the place they made their home was officially scheduled for a sheriff's auction. "What a day this has been," Clarence thought. "I suppose I should be afraid." He was somewhat surprised that losing the house seemed so unimportant to him. The enormity of other bills which he would never be able to repay loomed over him, but there was no fear in his spirit, only gratitude. "I've got my little girl." He didn't know what the future would hold, but he knew and trusted the awesome power of God. He believed that you could feel God's overwhelming presence in the silent moments that present themselves during a crisis or catastrophe. This was one of them. At this "moment", he was deeply grateful that God had spared Mandy's life. He had no clue when this storm would weaken, and when calm would return to their lives. He didn't know where his family would live and could not envision any specifics for the future fate of his family, But he understood God's promise of peace. He held tightly to that covenant of peace, which no earthly circumstance could break. *"And the peace of God, which passeth all understanding, shall keep your hearts and minds through Christ Jesus." (Philippians 4:7 KJV).* And this country boy knew one thing for certain; God would guide their ship to solid ground. In that promise, his faith remained anchored securely.

MANDY MANIA

"For your kingdom is an everlasting kingdom.
You rule throughout all generations.
The Lord always keeps his promises;
He is gracious in all he does."

— PSALM 145:13 NLT

I t was the eleventh hour. The Greens had sacrificed all that they possessed for love. The right hand of God was now moving silently, stirring its power within the unseen spiritual realm. People, places and events were in motion, all which would confirm the Green's faith in their Creator. *Galatians 6:2 "Help carry one another's burdens, and in this way you will obey the law of Christ." (GNT)* Unbeknown to the Greens, Beverly's sister, Jan, began contacting area news stations with the family's story, hoping more help would come if they could get the word out to their community through yes, a television station. Still, hope not failing, fellow church members planned to attend the auction to try and bid on the Green's home. The Sunday before the auction was to take place, pledges of $12,000 had been collected, exceeding the $10,000 minimum required to begin the bidding. Jan and her husband quietly worked behind the scenes to obtain another loan that the family could use to pay off a portion of the debt.

Two days before the auction, the call came to Jan's workplace. The message from the high school secretary interrupted her class. "There is a call from Channel 10's news director, from Columbus, waiting to be returned." This man, possibly an angel in disguise, was personally touched by the Green's plight and wanted to film the family's story for the television's evening news broadcast. By the time everything was put into place, it was the day before the auction. The crew from channel 10 arrived at the Green's home, ready to spend the day with the family, and meet Mandy. They sat in the living room of the Green's home with Clarence, Beverly and their children. Off camera, they shared tears with the family, while on camera, the crew recorded their emotions and personal accounts of their struggles. Their story would be spread to the large viewing audience on Channel 10's evening news broadcast. The Greens were once again trusting that God would see them through. They had no plan if their home was sold at auction. Their personal belongings were not packed for removal if they lost their house. They relied upon "the promise." Nothing more was needed.

Beverly was again reminded of the dream in which God spoke to her about saving their home through the Television. "The IRS told my husband that they would come and seize everything. But if it comes to that, we're determined. We will walk down the street together singing, because God has still given us so many things." "You are facing a bank foreclosure on your home tomorrow," the reporter stated to Clarence. "Yes, that's right." he replied. "It's got to be very frustrating for you." "Yes, to a certain degree, I guess it is. But I think my friends are more worried about that than I really am. I've got Mandy. We're still living, and we're happy. Even though we could possibly lose our home, it's not the most important thing in the world."

The entire day was spent interviewing and filming their story for the evening news. Walter, now 15 years old, shared his emotional thoughts surrounding Mandy's first day of school. "It's sort of like a dream that you never thought would come true." "Yet, it was always there and you were always hoping it would happen someday. She always wanted to ride the bus - she always wanted to know what it was like. It was her dream." As word of Mandy's story spread through the community, donations began coming in, even before the story aired. That evening, when their story was told, one man in particular was watching it with his daughter. They were both moved by compassion and the desire to help them from their hardship. The young daughter turned to her father. "Are you going to help them, Dad?" "Yes, I am!" he answered.

But, the Green family didn't own a TV. They didn't watch the story that was aired. They had family prayer, as always, and went to bed shortly thereafter; each of them quietly wondering what the next day would bring. Clarence was exhausted but sleep would not come. He felt both energized and emotionally drained by what had taken place that day. His wife and children were asleep. He knew the truth and comfort of God's Word, yet he still fought against the natural fear that arose within his heart. Closing his eyes and finding courage in God's Word and the promises that he knew to be true, Clarence began counting the seemingly endless miracles that God had done for his family. He smiled at his wife's words, "It's just been a parade of miracles." Clarence clung to God's spirit of courage and recalled, 2 Timothy 1:7, "For God has not given us a spirit of fear; but of power, and of love, and of a sound mind" (NKJV). Clarence felt God's presence and found strength and peace in the knowledge of this truth: although fear may come, it has no place of welcome within a heart of faith. His heart, along with his family, would be secure no matter what future days would bring. Sleep overtook him, as his humble and grateful spirit rested.

ANGELS FLY HELICOPTERS

"For all of God's promises have been fulfilled in Christ
With a resounding "Yes!"
And through Christ, our "Amen" (which means "Yes")
Ascends to God for his glory."

— 2 CORINTHIANS 1:20 NLT

In the face of pain that seared their soul, the Green family was not going to run away, quit or pass their responsibilities on to someone else; they were willing to face the personal loss. Their hearts had been broken, their spirits utterly poured out and yet, they stood steadfast in their faith. In the moments when we have nothing left, God steps in, and "stands in the gap."

Along the path of freedom from fear, it will always be some form of deliverance which releases the shackles that bind us. Sometimes the bonds that hold us captive are physical, as with the Greens' daughter, Mandy. Other times, though we have hope, we can be restrained by the cold hard facts and circumstances of our lives.

There are also moments when the bonds of fear are self-imposed. We cling to circumstances or false beliefs, simply because they are familiar signposts along our former lives of self destruction. A prisoner who has been set free, must take the first steps and walk through the door that has been unlocked and opened for him. God has offered freedom from fear to all of us. Today is the day. Walk through the door that has been opened. Sometimes, when God delivers us, it is in a still and quiet way; other times, after we have climbed the full height of the mountain, He sets us free to enjoy the view from the highest of heights. But always, He does it in such a way that there is no mistaking it for anything other than His great and mighty hand of power and grace moving on behalf of His children.

The door to freedom from fear was torn open for Clarence and Beverly. There is no mistaking the one who delivered them.

The morning of the auction finally arrived. Beverly kept the children occupied as they worked together to make a huge sign. *"THANK GOD FOR FRIENDS."* Each child was busy drawing their assigned letters on pieces of paper that would be strung together from one tree to another in their front yard. It was their expression of gratitude for the efforts of family and friends who had gathered around the Greens, giving their all to save their home. As this act of thankfulness was taking place, God's powerful hand continued moving, sight unseen, swiftly, but profoundly touching the hearts of more people. The family had no idea that "Mandy Mania" was taking over the community. Love is a contagious thing. Children from their community were now walking door to door, raising contributions for Mandy's medical care and to stop the auction. Young school mates contributed their lunch and allowance money. Firemen passed their hats in front of their fire stations and churches were collecting love offerings in the hope that it might help save the Green's home. But, there was more.

The phone rang. Clarence answered. It was one hour before the sale. The Greens knew that some of their family and friends were gathering at the courthouse this morning to support them. Channel 10 news was there to cover it. The message Clarence received over the phone both confused and distressed him. "The sale has been cancelled for the day." He was told that their house could not be transferred to a new owner until additional paperwork was completed. Chaos and confrontation had broken out in the courthouse between the IRS and the remaining lender bank, which held the other mortgage on the Green property. Walter turned to his father and asked, "Now what do we do?" Clarence answered softly. "We're still going to make the sign."

Later that afternoon, the Channel 10 news truck and crew returned to the Green's home. With their future and uncertainty still hanging in the balance, the family gathered again in their living room. Beverly sat close to her husband with Mandy on her lap. "Did you expect this type of outpouring of love?" the reporter asked. The tremendous support from their neighbors and friends, with the help of Channel 10, raised funds totaling $50,000. "No, we never expected this." Clarence said. "It reaffirms that God is real and that there's a God in Heaven that cares, who hears and answers prayer." "And, you've got a healthy little daughter there. That has to make you feel wonderful." "If I didn't have anything else, I've got everything today. I've got everything because we've got our family, we've got a big God that cares and whether or not we have the other things, it really doesn't matter." Clarence knew that the total due was much higher than the $50,000. "But, maybe," he thought, "maybe, this gift will buy us a little time to figure things out." The reporter broke through his thoughts. "Well, we've got some news for you this morning. The bank has cancelled the sheriff's sale and you can stay in your home." The Greens were stunned. "Is that right?" Clarence asked. Through tears and with joy, Beverly could only say, once again, "It's a big miracle. It's been a parade of miracles from day one." She was far past overwhelmed.

Watching the Green family's story, aired on Channel 10 news the previous evening, Bill Kraner, a multi-millionaire businessman and philanthropist, from their hometown of Newark, Ohio, was the gentleman who responded "yes" to his daughter's question. He answered the call to help this family, whom he had never met, and in doing so, said "yes" to a divine appointment which he never anticipated. Though he fiercely guarded his privacy, this man of great wealth and power arrived at the Green's home to introduce himself to the entire family. He couldn't wait to meet the people who had inspired and touched his heart with their story, face to face. Reaching for Clarence's hand, he gave his solemn promise, from one father to another. "No matter what happens, you will have a home to live in," he said. "If this house is not the right one, I'll buy one similar to it. And I am going to help take care of your other bills." As they gathered outside in the wake of what had taken place, the intense emotions held at bay earlier that day, burst through the dam of fear and uncertainty. Bill Kraner reached down to pick Mandy up and held her beneath the sign that the family had made. When he placed her down, Mandy looked up at her mother and said, "Mommy, that man was shaking!" When joy fills a heart, it jolts the entire body. *"Rejoice in the Lord always: and again I say, Rejoice!" (Philippians 4:4 KJV)* Rejoice and be glad!

Two weeks later, Mr. Kraner came to visit again. This time, he piloted and landed his private helicopter in the pasture next to the Green's home. He had spent the morning, first making a downpayment to the IRS with the money raised from the community, then paying the balance in cash, from his own money. He then flew back to the bank which held the first mortgage on the Green's home. He paid it in full. Finally, after paying off their second mortgage at another bank, he continued his helicopter journey to the Green's home. It was quite a scene. The Green children, especially the boys, were in awe, as the giant metal bird landed in their front yard's pasture. Bill Kraner was now divinely bound, by love and the touch of God, to the Green family. The two mortgage documents were ceremoniously burned in the pasture. Yet, more was to come. Bill Kraner, with the help of a few of the friends present, formed a plan. They surprised the family by "sneaking" a brand new minivan into their backyard while the Greens were distracted by his helicopter landing. Clarence and Beverly were stunned by his generosity. Their current minivan, with 160,000 miles on the odometer, many of which had been tallied during their life or death trips to the hospital with Mandy, was officially retired.

Clarence secretly made his way to the fire pit for a quiet moment. From there, he was able to take in the entire scene. He watched as his Bevie, holding Mandy, laughed with Mr. Kraner. The burden she bore for so long had been lifted. Clarence could see the joy light his bride's face. He wanted to mentally capture this moment in time. He glanced at each of his children. The boys were tossing a basketball around. Their faces could barely contain their emotions. Surrounded by friends and family, Clarence thought, "There is no man on earth more blessed than I am at this moment." He wished his dear friend and pastor could be there to witness the fulfillment of God's promise, to see his bold prayer answered. Pastor's Wilson's wife was sitting on the swing with Molly. The entire scene was far beyond any victory he could have imagined. The sound of celebration filled the air, and his heart, with a joy that he never thought possible.

Extending his hospitality far beyond "simple charity," Bill Kraner personally took the Greens, along with his wife and daughter, on his private jet to enjoy a vacation filled with the things which fairy tales are made of. They went to Disney World, fulfilling Beverly's dream. Bill Kraner wanted to personally ensure they enjoyed the freedom and fun of a family vacation. He didn't hold anything back. He rolled out a crimson red carpet for the Greens as they deplaned and stepped off of his plane in Florida. He didn't do it for public recognition or fanfare. It simply made him happy to give joy to this family who had been through so much anguish. He, himself, felt like a kid again. He personally gave the boys a giant Mickey Mouse and for the girls, a Minnie Mouse. "I thought I lived in Ohio, but I'm really living in a state of shock," Clarence said, watching his family as they enjoyed the magic of Disney World. "I hope I can turn things around a little bit so that I end up on the giving end."

For the first time in 5 years, their laughter was not clouded with the question, "How long will this last?" For the first time, in a long time, the uncertainty of their future wasn't clouded with struggle, doubt or fear. Their spirits were lifted in praise, trepidation was traded for joy, and peace replaced the terror of battle. They had Mandy, they had each other, they were debt free and they had their home.

27

GOD'S COUNTRY

Then He who sat on the throne said,
"Behold, I make all things new."
And He said to me, "Write, for these words are true and faithful."

— REVELATION 21:5 NKJV

Time stood still in the quietness of the hospital room. Melody refused to leave Mandy's side. The hospital had finally given permission for her to stay with Mandy in her room as long as she continued to be stable. She pulled the chair as close to Mandy as she could, laying her head next to her sister and wrapping herself in the blanket. "Can you hear me, Mandy?" Clarence had told the children that Mandy could hear them, even if she was unresponsive. Melody whispered, "I prayed for you, Mandy. I wanted a baby sister to play with and God answered my prayer. I can't lose you now." Melody sat and talked with Mandy, read stories to her and even watched movies on the hospital's television, hoping something would cause her to wake up. But, there was no response to encourage Melody's heart. The blips and beeps monitoring Mandy's vital signs were the only sounds that broke through the silence. Melody stayed, regardless.

By the time Mandy reached 6th grade, the doctors determined that her back was fixed at a 75 degree angle from another condition, scoliosis, or misalignment of her spine. This curvature, pushing her head toward her lungs, made it difficult for her to breathe. "The body brace isn't working. Mandy is losing weight and has gotten so tiny that if the scoliosis worsens, the pressure on Mandy's organs will be irreversible. "Mandy will not survive unless she has surgery," the doctors told Clarence and Beverly. "There is no way around it." Beverly and Clarence were filled with doubts about exposing Mandy to yet another procedure. There was much risk involved with surgery of this nature. With Mandy's history of bleeding, the odds of any relief or recovery from this condition were not in her favor. But without this surgery, the Green's would certainly lose their daughter. In the final analysis, they were faced with a Hobson's Choice. If they opposed the surgery, they would lose their daughter in due time. If they accepted the doctor's opinion and chose the surgery, Mandy at best, would survive with only a possibility of a full recovery. There were no other choices. Either way, the situation appeared fragile. In the end, after everything they'd been through, this uncertain and high risk surgery was scheduled and performed. Mandy was on the operating table for 12 hours and lost 17 pints of blood during the surgery. The Greens were faced with the prospect, once again, of losing their daughter. "God must have written a different ending to this story." Melody thought. "He must have another plan."

Laying in the ICU, Mandy could hear voices. She heard her family and thought, at one point, that she heard Mr. & Mrs. Kraner's voices, but she couldn't understand what they were saying. Mandy had never felt so much pain. Her entire body, from head to toe, was swollen. She couldn't move one muscle in her body. She was exhausted and didn't want to exert the effort to open her eyes. She could not continue this battle much longer. She was virtually unrecognizable.

Mandy was in a deep sleep, a place that seemed peaceful to her. Each time she drifted into this peaceful place more deeply, she heard Melody calling out to her. "Mandy! Mandy! Wake up!" But she could not. "Don't leave me Mandy, I need you!" Again, she heard Melody's voice calling to her from somewhere in the distance, but was unable to answer. There was calm and peace now as she felt herself moving beyond time to a place she had never seen, and yet was all at once familiar to her. In this place of knowing, she felt herself being surrounded by what might be described as clouds, but was more accurately, a gentle mist, engulfed by light. Within this place, there was peace, love and knowing - she was not afraid.

The shroud suddenly opened and gave way to light. "This is crazy beautiful." Mandy thought, "It's the brightest white that I've ever seen." She couldn't look away. It was a dazzling and complete illumination containing the fullness of every spectrum of color. Mandy was mesmerized by its purity and the indescribable joy it brought to her soul. She was in God's country. Mandy was able to see everything distinctly now, through spiritual eyes free from the blindness of pain or worldly corruption. She remained in this peaceful stillness for a time, free to linger or move on as she chose. Slowly, she began to see the vivid color of what appeared to be bright flowers. Each color was distinct in itself and at the same time, one with the other colors and the bright white that surrounded it all. "Everything is so crisp and intense." Mandy observed these colors, true and pure as if she was seeing them for the very first time. She heard a voice. "Mandy, please come back." Confused, Mandy continued to move toward the beautiful colors. She saw that they surrounded a gate which was opening as she moved closer. She didn't answer the voice that was calling her. She continued instead, toward the gate and stepped inside. It was perfection.

Mandy saw people walking and children playing. The further she looked, the more she was able to see the fullness of it all. She realized for the first time that she felt no pain. Wonder filled her soul as she felt welcomed there. She felt as if she was finally home again. She continued through the brightness, which calmed her spirit. She saw glowing lights, brighter than the light that surrounded her. The light that surrounded the images made them appear to glow from behind. It was the power of this light which created a bright shadow that reached far beyond their bodies. Were they angels, she wondered? They didn't have wings like she would have imagined, but the light was irresistible to her as she moved closer to them. Mandy felt engulfed on all sides, surrounded by God's loving presence. She felt the fullness of this love and finally recognized the One in the midst of it all. He looked different from the pictures she had seen. He didn't have long hair, but she couldn't stop looking into his eyes that held such great love for her. His eyes pierced hers, creating an absolute feeling of trust and knowing. Mandy wanted to run into his arms. Jesus smiled and held out his arms.

The voice once more called out to Mandy. "Mandy, don't leave me, don't leave me. I need you - you have to fight. I can't lose my little sister, I prayed for you for too long. Please don't leave me!" Melody saw Mandy move and continued to call to her. "Mandy, wake up! Watch this movie with me, it's so funny!" Mandy heard Melody now. "I'm trying, it's really hard, Melody. I'm so tired. There is so much pain." She looked again to Jesus. He put his arms down. His lips didn't move, but she heard him speak. "Mandy, it's ok. You can go live your life. It's all here for you - when you're ready to come home, I'll bring you right here. I'll be waiting for you." Mandy knew the pain she would have to face. She was exhausted beyond anything she had experienced, but she couldn't leave Melody. She could hear her again, begging her to open her eyes. "Have a drink of water, Mandy, " she pleaded.

Mandy opened her eyes, confused. She saw Melody hop up as she opened her eyes. "Mandy!", Melody exclaimed. "I'm thirsty, Melody," Mandy said weakly. Melody gave her a sip of water as the tears flowed freely from her. "What happened?" Mandy asked. "You kept coding, Mandy.", Melody said through her tears. "You kept coding and every time you did, I begged you to come back. I couldn't bear it if you left me. Where did you go?" "I'm not sure," Mandy said, "everything is a blur." Mandy knew what she had seen, but didn't dare tell. She knew she had seen the gates of Heaven, but it would be her secret. A special and intimate secret that allowed her to keep going, even now, in the midst of the pain which had returned.

Mandy could feel the weight of the rod within her back. It was only a few days after her surgery when the nurse came by with instructions. "Let's get you moving, Mandy." Mandy thought she must be crazy to think that she could move any part of her body amidst the pain which seemed to paralyze her. She stared at the nurse, but ultimately knew the choice she had to make. She chose this life. She chose this pain and she would choose whatever it took to recover. It would be a long road back. First, Mandy learned to move around with a walker. At a later point, the walker was tossed away, and Mandy learned how to walk on her own. All of it was breathtakingly painful. But Mandy would not give up.

This has always been Mandy's story; pick yourself up and keep going. Whatever life has thrown at her, she has overcome with the support of her faith and her family. If you tell her she can't do something, she will be the first to prove you wrong. Doctors said she wouldn't survive. Then, they said she would never walk. Teachers that never thought she would graduate were surprised and thankful that she did. Mandy graduated High School with honors and went on to obtain her pharmacy technician certification. Doctors said she would never have children. Mandy proved them wrong, too. Today, she has two beautiful and healthy daughters. All these things, in the end, are not surprising. With God, all things are possible for those who believe and abide by His word.

Mandy was given an opportunity to see what lies beyond this visible world. Yet, she chose to live her life, and share her story in the physical world so that others would know that through the difficult days of challenge that life brings, there is always a place of peace that awaits them. "God is always there." Mandy says. "When you're in the middle of something, and you don't see the way out, know that God is there and walk that path of faith. There is a place of eternal strength that is always available to each one of us." He has delivered us fully, through the sacrifice of His Son. *Ephesians 2:4: "But because of his great love for us, God, who is rich in mercy, made us alive with Christ even when we were dead in transgressions—it is by grace you have been saved." (NIV1984).*

In God's Country

Take off your shoes
A soft voice calls
The kingdom is at hand

Splendor and majesty
Eternal and unfailing
The voice of creation calls the free

In the kingdom
His presence dwells
All is Holy in this land

In the known
And in mystery
All creatures breathe

From East to West
Every corner of earth
High above and underneath

The grace of One
Goes before all
His kingdom is at hand
There is now, a calling
A rising, if you will
An invitation to victory

Your story unfolds
Written before time
In God's Country

28

REFLECTIONS

"And what more could I say to convince you...?"

— HEBREWS 11:32 TPT

"Well, it sure was a lot of fun to have that 'big bird' land in the pasture!," Clarence said. "One day it seems like your life is full of troubles and then it flip-flops and here you are almost a celebrity!" Beverly was a rock of solid faith for the Green family through it all. "And it was just a miracle - everything from the beginning to the end." She recalls the prayer that she had prayed. "Lord, if you want us to keep Mandy, make it in such a fashion that only you can get glory for it." Beverly is as sentimental as she is faithful. "I kept the ashes of those mortgage papers sitting on our piano as a reminder of what God delivered us from and will keep them there for the rest of my days." Clarence offered, "It did take a while to come down off our big cloud as we rolled back in. But, what a wonderful ride, and it seemed like we had climbed the stairs from below the bottom to get to above the top." "You know, you have your dreams. And I had my dreams as a young boy that Daddy and I would be working together back on the farm."

As is true for most of us, the story that God authored in Clarence's life, each moment personally etched and carved with love, is quite different from what he would have written for himself. His story is a gift filled with moments that caused him to hold his breath and moments that took his breath away. "But, oh what a wonderful trip!" Clarence exclaims. And he can say nothing except that he has lived beyond his dreams. Although some of the challenges were so hard, he didn't think he could endure them. "The mountaintops that we have been able to enjoy have been absolutely breathtaking." He's still so excited to this very day. "It ain't over yet. What's around the next corner? What's around the next hill? There are still some great victories out there to be won." " And I would love to finish with a grand finale!" "Just prop me up one last time. I want to leave here shoutin'! Giving God the glory and praise for the ride we have enjoyed will be my grand finale. So, if you hear a lot of noise, that could be the old man Green passing on!"

And God has given Clarence what he hoped for, long ago, at Disney. "I hope I can turn things around a little bit so that I end up on the giving end." This is it. Their story, shared with you - and me. To encourage all of us to press on, in faith, to run the good race, proclaiming the glory of God until we pass the finish line.

> *For there is not enough time to tell you of the faith of Gideon, Barak, Samson, Jephthah, David, Samuel, and the prophets.*
> *Through faith's power they conquered kingdoms and established true justice. Their faith fastened onto their promises and pulled them into reality!*
> *It was faith that shut the mouth of lions, put out the power of raging fire, and caused many to escape certain death by the sword.*

*Although weak, their faith imparted power to make them strong!
Faith sparked courage within them and they became mighty warriors
    in battle, pulling armies from another realm into battle array.
Faith-filled women saw their dead children raised in resurrection
    power."*

— HEBREWS 11:32-35 (TPT)

EPILOGUE

"Dear friends, let us love one another, because love comes from God.
Whoever loves is a child of God and knows God.
Whoever does not love does not know God, for God is love.
And God showed his love for us by sending his only Son into the
world,
so that we might have life through him."

— JOHN 4:7-9 GNT

The remarkable events in the lives of the Green family were authored long ago. Weaving through the seemingly catastrophic events in their lives, was grace upon grace - and a glimpse into the mystery of God's unfolding work of love in the lives of his children. We saw God's hand at work time and time again. "A parade of miracles," as Beverly always said. Yes, a parade of miracles continuing to this day to bring forth His ultimate plan, divine purpose and this love letter to you. Perhaps that statement seems too forward - or a bit too bold - but possibly, the time for boldness and fearless faith has come.

Most times, we don't recognize God's work in our lives. But, he walks among us. His works are often hidden in plain sight, 'dressed up like ordinary'. The Greens are just ordinary people. They could have been the family living right down the street from any of us. We might not notice anything extraordinary about the people that God chooses to accomplish His purpose. Yet, we stumble along until there is a turning point. A decision that has to be made that is consistent with God's word. When we come face to face with our own struggles, powerlessness and hopelessness, we need only reach our hand out to him for his blessings and salvation. If we lay down our burdens before the healer who reigns, we will witness the fullness of His grace, mercy and healing in abundance. God beautifully promises in *Isaiah 61:3*: *"To all who mourn in Israel, He will give a crown of beauty for ashes, a joyous blessing instead of mourning, festive praise instead of despair. In their righteousness, they will be like great oaks that the Lord has planted for His own glory."* *(NLT) Selah.*

God has not stopped working. Amen. We are reminded, in a most precious truth: *"See, I have inscribed you on the palms of My hands",* Isaiah 49:16 *(NKJV).* God's memory is everlasting. He will never forsake us. We may forget for a moment, but God, in His love, reminds us that He cares and it is the abiding love of God that enables us to see beyond our circumstances. God is perfect, as is all He creates.

Through the ages and to this day, His hand can be seen in the lives of His children. Day by day, there is sufficient grace to carry us through the trials, joys, sorrows and laughter of life. Each sunrise brings the opportunity to witness - and testify - to the works that He is doing. We all have a story. *You* have a story. From childhood to adulthood, you have experienced the good, the bad, the joy and the heartaches of this world. The book of your life holds living power and is waiting to be told; to encourage others, spread hope and declare grace boldly over the lives of others for such a time as this. God will not leave you where you are. He will not leave you where you were in the past. Nothing in your life is wasted. Everything you have experienced has a purpose. For His purpose – for His glory - and for your part in this eternal, never ending story of love; that your light would shine so others may witness your victory.

And now, may the peace of God which passeth all understanding guide your heart, fill your soul with rest and ignite the flame of endless, eternal and abiding love within you. It is greatly needed now, more than ever.

May God bless you and keep you.

Dedicated to Beverly J. "Bevie" Green (1945-2018).

Made in United States
Orlando, FL
24 November 2021

10705210R00075